PROFILING: A User's Manual

Also from Stanley Thornes (Publishers) Ltd:

A Teacher's Guide to Assessment   D. S. Frith
                                     H. G. Macintosh

PROFILING:
A User's Manual

David GARFORTH

Henry MACINTOSH

STANLEY THORNES (PUBLISHERS) LTD

First published in 1986 by:
Stanley Thornes (Publishers) Ltd
Old Station Drive
Leckhampton
CHELTENHAM GL53 0DN
England

British Library Cataloguing in Publication Data

Garforth, David
　　Profiling a user's manual.
　　1. Students – Great Britain – Rating of
　　I. Title　　II. Macintosh, H.G.
　　371.2'64　　　LB1117

　　ISBN 0-85950-230-9

Typeset by Schooltext, CHELTENHAM, GL53 8BS
Printed and bound in Great Britain at the Alden Press Ltd, Oxford.

STANLEY THORNES

INCORPORATING HULTON EDUCATIONAL PUBLICATIONS
AND STAM PRESS

STANLEY THORNES (Publishers) Ltd.
Old Station Drive, Leckhampton.
Cheltenham, Gloucestershire. GL53 0DN England
Telephone: Cheltenham (0242) 584429   Telex: 43592

Date as Invoice

Dear Sir/Madam

Thank you for your recent order requesting
supply under our Inspection Copy Service.

We regret this title is not available under
this scheme, not being suitable for class
adoption.

However, we are sending it 'On Approval', but
must insist on payment or return of book
strictly within 28 days. Thank you.

Yours faithfully

D C Steel
Trade Manager

Enc

Directors: S E Thornes   R M Kendall   M M van de Weijer   M J van Dalen
EDUCATIONAL PUBLISHERS   Registered in England No. 108 3899   VAT Reg. No. 302 3194 07

CONTENTS

1 What is a profile?   1

The first chapter provides:

– a *description* for profiles and records of achievement
– information regarding the scope of the possible *contents*
   of profiles
– information and examples relating to the difference between
   student-centred profiles and *course-related profiles.*

2 Why have profiles been developed?   11

The chapter outlines the reasons for the recent widespread
development of profiles and identifies both *external factors*
and *internal factors.*

3 A plan for development   14

Schools and colleges need to decide whether they will adapt
an existing profile or design their own.

A plan for *design, development* and *implementation* is
provided.

4 Profile planning: institutional self-evaluation   17

During the planning stage it is important for schools and
colleges to consider the question 'Where are we now?' in
addition to the question 'Where do we wish to go?' It is
accepted that many publications already exist that can provide
assistance for teachers in any evaluation of present practices
in the areas of the curriculum, the recording and reporting

policies and the pastoral structure. The chapter, therefore, provides some guidelines for evaluation of the *assessment policies and practices.*

Successful development is more likely to be achieved if issues are agreed in advance around several characteristics. These are:

(1) What are the main purposes of the profile?
(2) Who is to be profiled?
(3) What is to be assessed?
(4) How is the assessment to be undertaken?
(5) Who is to be involved in the assessment process?
(6) How are the results of the assessment to be recorded?

It is suggested that the profile may consist of four possible components:

– *subject assessment*
– *cross-curricular skills*
– *personal and social skills*
– *achievements and experiences.*

For each of these components, three questions are posed and examples are offered to reveal the scope of possible responses:

(1) What are the criteria for assessment?
(2) What is the most appropriate method of assessment for each of the chosen criteria?
(3) How is the information to be recorded?

This chapter considers recent trends in assessment which reflect upon profile development. In particular, attention is given to:

– performance criteria
– the extension of information provided about student
  performance
– the concept of 'fitness for purpose'

The chapter also considers five issues relating to assessment methods:

(1) Asking the 'right' question
(2) Assignments and log books
(3) Descriptive assessment
(4) Observation
(5) Evaluating responses

ACKNOWLEDGEMENTS

The authors and publishers would like to thank the following for permission to reproduce material:

Barnsley Metropolitan Borough Council
Bosworth College, Desford, Leicestershire
City and Guilds of London Institute
Clwyd County Council
Department of Education and Science
Evesham School, Worcestershire
Helston School, Cornwall
Lea Manor High School, Luton, Bedfordshire
Inner London Education Authority
Norton Priory School, Runcorn, Cheshire
Pilgrim School Bedford
Royal Society of Arts
Metropolitan Borough of Solihull
Sutton Centre, Sutton-in-Ashfield, Nottinghamshire
Suffolk County Council (Copyright Suffolk County Council 1986 and published by permission of Suffolk County Council)
University of Oxford Delegacy of Local Examinations
Victorian Institute of Secondary Education, Melbourne, Australia
West Midlands Examination Board
Wiltshire County Council

The authors would also like to express their appreciation to Mrs Mary E. Waldman, and the Dorset County Assessment Team (John Blanchard, Len Brazier, Les Cowling, David Hanson and Frank Newhofer).

ABBREVIATIONS

The terms listed below are given in full and in abbreviated form when they first occur, and after that in abbreviated form only:

Assessment of Performance Unit	APU
City and Guilds of London Institute	CGLI
Certificate of Pre-Vocational Education	CPVE
Department of Education and Science	DES
Further and Higher Education	FHE
General Certificate of Secondary Education	GCSE
Graded Objectives for Achievement in Language Skills	GOALS
Inner London Education Authority	ILEA
In Service Education and Training	INSET
Local Education Authority	LEA
Oxford Certificate of Educational Achievement	OCEA
Royal Society of Arts	RSA
Southern Regional Examination Board	SREB
Technical and Vocational Education Initiative	TVEI
Victorian Institute of Secondary Education	VISE

INTRODUCTION

'The Secretaries of State hope that it will be possible by the end of the decade to establish throughout England and Wales arrangements under which all young people in secondary schools will have records of achievement and will take with them when they leave school a summary document of record prepared within a framework of national policy which leaves scope for local variations.'

Records of Achievement: A Statement of Policy
Department of Education and Science, Welsh Office, July 1984

If this hope is to become a reality, then over the next few years all secondary school teachers will be closely involved in developing and operating schemes to record student progress and achievements.

This book aims to be a concise, accessible, jargon-free introduction to profiles and records of achievement for people who have no specialist training in assessment. It is aimed primarily at those who teach and train young people between the ages of 11 and 18 in schools, colleges, or any other institution where organised programmes of education or training are provided. This does not mean that profiles are only applicable to a particular age group or to particular institutions. Profiling has been used for many years in primary and special education and in Manpower Services Commission Schemes and is becoming a part of everyday life for managers, lecturers and tutors in Colleges of Further Education. Profiles are relevant to part-time and full-time students and in the workplace as well as in schools, colleges or universities. A profiling system makes credit transfer*, progression and continuity in education easier and should therefore be used as widely as possible throughout formal education.

* Credit transfer is the acceptance by one agency of achievement publicly acknowledged by another, despite differences in the agencies' requirements.

The book aims to provide practical information and advice in answer to three main questions

(1) What is a profile?

(2) What does the profiling system have to offer?

(3) How might a profiling system be developed and operated effectively?

The major part of the book will deal with the third question to help bridge the gap between theory and practice and to enable profiles to develop successfully in the real world of day-to-day teaching and learning.

Chapter 1

WHAT IS A PROFILE?

You will have already realised that both the terms *records of achievement* and *profiles* have been used in the Introduction. For the purposes of this book the two terms are largely interchangeable, encompassing

a formative process of recording information which could assist someone while still a student, and

a summative statement of achievements made on completion of studies.

DESCRIPTIONS OF PROFILES AND PROFILING

A profile is a system of recording information derived from assessment and usually, but not exclusively, about individuals. Profiling is the process by which a profile or record of achievement is produced. These definitions draw attention to two important facts.

(1) Many profiles already exist. They range from examination certificates, using grades and nothing else, to school reports comprising verbal descriptions and usually some reference to a class position obtained by a grade or percentage score. Such descriptions tend to be general although on occasions there may be different grades or statements for aspects or components of the performance or course.

(2) Profiles are not of themselves methods of assessment. They make use of assessment in a wide variety of formal and informal methods. They are therefore only as full and varied as the information they present and differ from each other in (a) content, and (b) presentation, which will influence the recording process by focusing on certain features and ignoring others.

THE CONTENTS OF PROFILES

Whatever form it takes, a profile ought to contain three basic elements.

(1) A list of items forming the basis of the assessment. These may be called 'criteria' and may be in the form of a list of skills or qualities or may be embodied within a course description.

(2) A means of indicating the level and/or nature of performance reached for each item in this list. Almost any means can be used including marks, grades, percentages, histograms, bar graphs, statements and descriptive assessments.

(3) An indication of the evidence used to arrive at the description provided. This element is unfortunately often ignored but it is vital to indicate the context in which a particular skill is assessed if the nature of its performance is to be fully understood.

These three elements can be seen in the Progress Profile Report of the City and Guilds of London Institute (CGLI) shown on pages 3–4. The level of performance for each item is identified by indicating which of the five boxes or stages contains the most appropriate statement. The tutor uses the blank section to show in what context the skill was displayed and to indicate the kind of evidence that produced that statement.

STUDENT-CENTRED PROFILES

We hope that we have already shown you profiling's potential for improving the information about individuals and/or their performance. This information can be valuable in many ways: it can be student-centred or course-related and can define achievement against an extremely wide range of objectives.

The Secretaries of State clearly see profiles as student-centred for recording a comprehensive picture of student progress and achievements across a wide spectrum of activities

'The Secretaries of State believe that the internal processes of reporting, recording and discussion between teacher and pupil should cover a

City and Guilds of London Institute

Progress

Main Activities:

	ABILITIES	EXAMPLES OF ABILITIES
COMMUNICATION	TALKING AND LISTENING	
	READING	
	WRITING	
PRACTICAL & NUMERICAL	USING EQUIPMENT	
	NUMERACY (I)	
SOCIAL	WORKING IN A GROUP	
	ACCEPTING RESPONSIBILITY	
DECISION-MAKING	PLANNING	
	COPING	
	OBTAINING INFORMATION	

ADDITIONAL	WORKING WITH CLIENTS	
	USING SIGNS AND DIAGRAMS	
	NUMERACY (II)	
	SAFETY	
	COMPUTER APPRECIATION	

Profile

Profile No..........

Name of Centre and Course ....

Period covered by this Review   From ....   To ....

Signed ....   Signed ....

(Trainee/Student)   (Supervisor/Tutor)

PROGRESS IN ABILITIES

Can make sensible replies when spoken to	Can hold conversations and can take messages	Can follow and give simple descriptions and explanations	Can communicate effectively with a range of people in a variety of situations	Can present a logical and effective argument. Can analyse others' arguments
Can read words and short phrases	Can read straightforward messages	Can follow straightforward written instructions and explanations	Can understand a variety of forms of written materials	Can select and judge written materials to support an argument
Can write words and short phrases	Can write straightforward messages	Can write straightforward instructions and explanations	Can write reports describing work done	Can write a critical analysis using a variety of sources
Can use equipment safely to perform simple tasks under guidance	Can use equipment safely to perform a sequence of tasks after demonstration	Can select and use suitable equipment and materials for the job, without help	Can set up and use equipment to produce work to standard	Can identify and remedy common faults in equipment
Can count and match objects, can recognise numbers	Can add and subtract whole numbers to solve problems	Can use × and ÷ to solve whole number problems	Can add, subtract and convert decimals and simple fractions	Can multiply and divide decimals and simple fractions
Can cooperate with others when asked	Can work with other members of the group to acheive common aims	Can understand own position and results of own actions within a group	Can be an active and decisive member of a group	Can adopt a variety of roles in a group
Can follow instructions for simple tasks and carry them out under guidance	Can follow instructions for simple tasks and carry them out independently	Can follow a series of instructions and carry them out independently	Can perform a variety of tasks effectively given minimal guidance	Can assume responsibility for delegated tasks and take initiative
Can identify the sequence of steps in everyday tasks, with prompting	Can describe the sequence of steps in a routine task, after demonstration	Can choose from given alternatives the best way of tackling a task	Can modify/extend given plans/routines to meet changed circumstances	Can create new plans/ routines from scratch
Can cope with everyday activities	Can cope with everyday problems. Seeks help if needed	Can cope with changes in familiar routines	Can cope with unexpected or unusual situations	Can help others to solve problems
Can ask for needed information	Can find needed information with guidance	Can use standard sources of information	Can extract and assemble information from several given sources	Can show initiative in seeking and gathering information from a wide variety of sources
Can help someone to carry out clients' requests	Can carry out clients' requests under supervision	Can carry out clients' requests without supervision	Can anticipate and fulfil clients' needs from existing resources	Can suggest realistic improvements to services for clients
Can recognise everyday signs and symbols	Can make use of simple drawings, maps, timetables	Can make use of basic graphs, charts, codes technical drawings, with help	Can interpret and use basic graphs, charts and technical drawings unaided	Can construct graphs and extract information to support conclusions
Can estimate answers to tasks involving whole numbers decimals and simple fractions	Can calculate percentages and averages	Can solve problems involving simple ratios and proportions	Can express a problem in terms of a simple formula and solve it	
Can remember safety instructions	Can explain the need for safety rules	Can spot safety hazards	Can apply safe working practices independently	
Can recognise everyday uses of computers	Can use keyboard to gain access to data	Can enter data into the system using existing programs	Can identify potential applications for computers	

pupil's progress and activities across the whole educational programme of the school, both in the classroom and outside, and possibly activities outside the school as well . . .

The summary document of record which young people take with them when leaving school or college will need to include two main components:

i) Information, other than academic successes, which throws light on personal achievements and characteristics.

ii) Evidence of attainments in academic subjects and practical skills, including any graded results in public examinations.'

The *National Profiling Network** shows that the majority of school profiles follow this general pattern. The summary-type (summative) Statement of Pupil Achievement from Suffolk County Council provides a good illustration of this.

* The National Profiling Network, c/o Advisory Service, County Hall, Dorchester DT1 1XJ

SUFFOLK COUNTY COUNCIL
EDUCATION COMMITTEE

STATEMENT OF PUPIL ACHIEVEMENT

. . . . .School

> This statement is based on a Profile which was designed to help pupils identify their strengths and weaknesses and encourage them to improve their performance.
>
> It has been completed by the school and the pupil named below and provides a summary of that pupil's qualities, activities and achievements, as well as a record of the subjects studied.

Name of Pupil . . . .

Date of Birth . . . .

Head's Signature . . . .

Duration of the Record . . . .

County Education Officer: Mr D G Graham, MA

ATTENDANCE

Year 3			Year 4			Year 5		

Tutor's comments (if needed)

Year 3 ....

Year 4 ....

Year 5 ....

Date ....

COURSE OF STUDY

Year 3	Year 4	Year 5	Exam Level

Examinations already taken with results if known:

Date	Subject	Level	Grade

STATEMENT OF ACHIEVEMENTS

This statement is made by the pupil and indicates those items which he or she wishes especially to highlight.

Interests, including leisure activities:

My favourite interest is birdwatching. I go out fairly regularly at the weekends to birdwatch just outside   , sometimes further afield. I am in the   member's group of the R.S.P.B. and attend most of their meetings. I am interested in British castles and cathedrals, as well as ancient history, mythology, geography, architecture and the land of Wales. I read a lot of books and often listen to music, from pop to classical. I enjoy watching natural history and sports on T.V. and I cycle and play tennis with friends.

Experiences of school life and work:

At school, I enjoy most of my subjects, especially biology, geography, maths and latin. I have passed my maths and English 'O' levels and, with my progress and mock results, I expect to gain good grades in all my subjects. In the last two years, I have been on a trip to Greece and one to Snowdonia with the school. During my fortnight work experience, I worked at the Development Plan division at   Borough Council. The work I did, involving a shopping survey and drawing up maps, was very interesting and it was very worthwhile.

Personal qualities:

I am determined in my work and dependable. I am polite and punctual, and I am a fairly good listener. I can work in a group as long as I have some influence on its organisation. I can follow directions and can organise myself and, generally, others. I am able to plan ahead and work to a deadline. I am reasonably artistic, neat and put great pride into my work. I can learn quickly, communicate fairly well and work easily with money and numbers.

Date . . . .

Pupil's Signature . . . .

Tutor's Signature . . . .

TUTOR'S REVIEW

Pupil's Name _____

.... has received all of his five years secondary education at .... High School where, in the past two years, he has followed G.C.E. courses in all his major subjects, and some additional ones as well. He is exceptionally gifted academically and is expected to obtain excellent grades in all of his examinations. He has, in the fourth year, already achieved good 'O' level passes in English Language and Literature and an 'A' in Mathematics. He has used some of the time this early success has given him in studying other subjects and it is particularly commendable that he is to attempt the examinations in History and Music this year. It would be impossible to overpraise the effort and conscientiousness which he puts into all of his class work.

It is not only in this area, however, that he is outstanding. He has assisted the school at many evening functions, by helping in the form room and by serving not only as an efficient and reliable prefect, but also as the class representative to the Prefects' Council where he is, with others, responsible for organising the prefects' duties.

Although undoubtedly studious he is interested in some sports and at school is commended for the intelligence, thought and skill which are displayed in this area of activity.

His leisure pursuits are active too, especially his interest in birdwatching and it is an indication of his total involvement in whatever he undertakes that he attends the R.S.P.B. meetings both indoor and in the field. He is interested in buildings from an artistic, architectural and historical point of view and takes pleasure in studying and listening to all types of music from classical to 'pop'.

For his two weeks' Work Experience in the fourth year he was employed in the Planning Department of .... Borough Council. Here he was engaged in responsible tasks normally carried out by students on vacation, surveying the town and noting the trends particularly in the shopping areas. He enjoyed this work, combining as it did social service, observation and responsibility and might consider it as a possible career in the future.

As can be supposed, he enjoys excellent relations with the staff and he also has a loyal group of friends. Quiet in his manner, he is totally reliable and trustworthy and his appearance and manner are excellent. His attendance and punctuality records are second to none and all in all he has been a tremendous credit to himself and to his family, and the school will be the poorer for his going.

We shall watch his future career with interest, for people with his skills of management allied to intelligence and integrity are rare and will be much needed in tomorrow's world.

Tutor's Signature ....

Date ....

COURSE-RELATED PROFILES

There are also some national course-related profiles whose number could increase as a result of developments in the Certificate of Pre-Vocational Education (CPVE), Technical and Vocational Education Initiative (TVEI) and the General Certificate of Secondary Education (GCSE). An example of a course-related profile is the Royal Society of Arts (RSA) Certificate of Vocational Preparation. The assessment objectives are identified clearly with the teaching objectives of the course listed in the form of the Profile Certificates. The information recorded in the profile consists of a series of statements of what the student should be able to do as a result of following the course. The objectives which the student successfully achieves are recorded on the final summative certificate.

FORM OF THE PROFILE CERTIFICATES

Clerical and Distribution Courses
The candidate is able to:

COMMUNICATION
List, select and organise information using alphabetical order.
Use accurate spelling and punctuation.
Draft simple letters and memos using appropriate layout.
Follow oral and written instructions.
Use the telephone as an effective means of communication.
Abstract relevant information from messages and transmit this in the appropriate spoken or legible written form.
Complete a variety of forms.
Use everyday reference books.

NUMERACY
Add, subtract, multiply and divide with reference to whole numbers and money.
List, select, check and transfer numerical information accurately.
Undertake simple calculations with reference to time.
Undertake simple calculations with reference to weights and measures.
Undertake simple calculations using percentages.
Undertake simple calculations involving commonly used fractions and their conversion to decimals.
Take cash payments and give correct change.
Read and understand commonly used tables, ready reckoners, diagrams and charts.
Estimate with reference to time, space and quantity.
Use a calculator with the ability to estimate the answer in advance.

CAREER AND PERSONAL DEVELOPMENT
Establish and maintain working relationships with individuals and with groups.
Carry out the tasks involved in all stages of the job selection procedures.
Find and use appropriate sources of help and advice.
Examine his/her own interests, talents and values in relationship to the world of work.
Understand some of the rights and duties of an adult in society.
Analyse one job in terms of the skills, training, qualifications, prospects, hours, conditions and likely pay involved and its availability and inter-dependence on other jobs.

Clerical Course Only

HANDLING MAIL
Sort and distribute mail.
Collate and check contents of envelopes.
Use a variety of equipment common in the mail room.
Make postable packets and parcels with correct and legible addresses.
Weigh parcels and packages to calculate stamps needed.
Use franking machines.

RECORD KEEPING
Use alphabetical, numerical, subject and geographical systems of classifying material.
Sort and sequence card indexes and cross-reference material for filing.
Select information as required and transfer it onto or into dockets, forms, invoices, cards, books etc.
Write orders, bills and receipts.
Retrieve information as required from files and records.
Identify the uses and sources of computer- based information.

OFFICE MACHINERY
Select, and use as appropriate, a range of reprographic equipment and materials including carbons, ink duplicators and photocopiers.
Use collators and staplers.
Demonstrate familiarity with alpha and numeric keyboards.
Type accurately envelopes and simple memos.

TELEPHONE AND RECEPTION SKILLS
Make and receive telephone calls responding appropriately to people and situations.
Receive and record messages accurately and neatly and distribute them promptly.
Use simple switchboards.
Give directions clearly and concisely.
Complete appointment books, message sheets and related records.
Converse appropriately with waiting callers.

SECURITY, HEALTH AND SAFETY
State in simple terms the relevant obligations of the employer and employee regarding health, hygiene and safety.
Identify hazards in work situations.
Follow proper procedures in emergencies e.g. fire, theft, illness, accident.

Chapter 2

WHY HAVE PROFILES BEEN DEVELOPED?

The recent widespread development of profiles in schools and colleges has resulted from a combination of internal and external factors.

EXTERNAL FACTORS

Inadequate information about pupil performance provided by public examinations

This has long been a cause for concern because public examinations results are the only formal and 'neutral' evidence of attainment for most young people leaving full-time education. Since the Norwood Report in 1944, virtually all major reports on secondary education have referred to the need for information in addition to that provided by public examinations. Many schools have therefore produced records of achievement for students leaving full-time education declaring their individual achievements and experiences across a spectrum of activities. In some schools these were seen to have particular advantages for those students who would not benefit from the results of public examinations. The principle that records of achievement should be available for all students is now widely accepted and is part of government policy.

Increased large-scale long-term youth unemployment

This has forced curriculum review on schools and colleges so that greater emphasis is now being placed on an individual's personal qualities and characteristics and on the identification, description and assessment of clusters of basic, preferably transferable, skills that young people should acquire to make them more easily employable.

INTERNAL FACTOR

The potential of profiling to assist the learning process

Although the two external factors have been powerful agents for change many see the major benefit of profiling as its capacity to assist a student's learning process. In the use of assessment there has been a marked shift of emphasis away from grading and labelling towards diagnosis and evaluation. To achieve such a shift in emphasis it has been necessary to reconsider the basis of assessment and to move away from emphasising differences between individuals and promoting negative comparisons towards stressing positive performance against defined criteria or objectives. This is called *a shift from norm to criterion referencing.* All current British examination reform proposals show this trend and it has been most notable in recent developments in Scotland.

Such a shift will have a radical effect on classroom teaching both in the preparation of the curriculum objectives and in the uses made of assessment and much greater emphasis will be placed on diagnosis and evaluation in teaching/learning strategies and course design. In this way assessment becomes an essential tool to assist learning rather than an unavoidable intrusion on classroom teaching.

Profiling is more than an alternative and improved system of national certification. The introduction of a well-designed profiling system has wide-ranging and extremely significant implications for

institutions
motivation
relationships between teachers, students and courses
teaching and assessment styles
curriculum patterns
guidance programmes
recording systems
staff training.

Work on profiles within schools and colleges has already led to significant reappraisal of assessment techniques by placing greater emphasis on assessment over a period of time and on the use of more informal assessment by observation. It has also meant that more people – including the students – are involved in the assessment process itself and has drawn attention to how assessments should be reported to the various people who receive them.

Even where planning is still taking place, profiling discussions have rapidly led to curriculum reappraisal. It has become clear to many teachers that the development of criteria for assessment first of all needs far clearer definitions of what students should learn. Assessment is therefore part of the teaching and learning process.

TYPES OF PROFILE

You will already realise that there could be a significant clash of interests between those profiles that mainly look inwards and those that mainly look outwards. *Inward-looking profiles* place their emphasis on continuous diagnosis and evaluation for the individual, group or school concerned. These are usually called *formative profiles*. *Outward-looking profiles* are ones which place their emphasis on end-of-course evaluation and providing information for people outside school such as employers and staff in further and higher education establishments. These are usually called *summative profiles*.

This same distinction was made in a slightly different way by the Scottish Vocational Preparation Unit in its publication 'Assessment in Youth Training; Made to Measure?' (1982), which called these two types of profile *records* and *reports*. A record is evidence from which outsiders can make judgements and is therefore open. A report is a judgement which outsiders can take as evidence and is therefore closed. The unit sees the majority of profiles as reports (albeit extended ones) and considers that their use is being inappropriately and inadequately exploited.

In practice there will always be pressure to make the maximum use of information particularly when it has taken a lot of time and effort to produce. Profile design must be concerned with presenting more positive and comprehensive information about individuals and their attributes so that information is readily accessible and easy to use for a wide variety of purposes.

Chapter 3

A PLAN FOR DEVELOPMENT

The remainder of this book deals with how to set about creating and operating a profiling system.

CHOOSING A PROFILE

The first decision to be made is: *What is the most appropriate profile to be developed and operated?* Schools and colleges can either

adapt an existing national, regional or local scheme, or

design their own profile.

There will be advantages in adapting a profile which enjoys credibility nationally particularly if it has undergone extensive piloting. But there may be even greater advantages for curriculum and staff development when a school or college designs its own profile.

Ultimately, an individual school or college must represent the most appropriate unit for the operation of the profiling system and must play a major part in its construction. There are three major reasons for this.

(1) Many profiles are simply concerned with enhancing the description of individuals or their performance. A well-designed profiling system helps to

(a) promote the curriculum objectives of the institution

(b) assist in the evaluation of the success of those objectives, and

(c) provide support for the individual student in the achievement of the objectives.

Assessment thus assists the learning process. A profile must be designed to relate to the specific curriculum objectives of the course or institution. Where a profile is restricted in its breadth or balance in interpreting particular curriculum objectives, it will fulfil only part of its potential and may become a bureaucratic imposition upon busy teachers. The evidence revealed by the profile must be of direct and immediate benefit to teachers and pupils because it is clearly related to the learning objectives of the course.

(2) Each educational establishment is unique. Its individuality will continue because the specific practical interpretation of curriculum objectives rests with the teachers in that particular school or college and its ethos depends on the interaction between individual teachers and unique students. The profile should thus take account of the ethos of the institution where it operates.

(3) The profile must take account of the assessment experience and expertise of the staff. Teachers must feel confident and competent to operate the scheme if its full potential is to be realised.

For these reasons the question of how to create and operate a profiling system will be dealt with almost entirely in terms of the individual school or college.

This is not to say that a school could not adapt someone else's scheme or use one being developed regionally to its benefit. The key word however needs to be *adapt* and not 'adopt'. It is vital to discover what implications any scheme will have for the school or college and to see how it relates to existing objectives for a particular course or indeed for the institution as a whole. A well-designed profiling system for an individual school or college can produce major benefits for it and the community it serves but only if there is careful planning and thorough preparation both at departmental and institutional level before implementation.

DESIGN, DEVELOPMENT AND IMPLEMENTATION

There are six essential stages in the design, development and implementation of a profiling system.

(1) A systematic programme for institutional self-evaluation

(2) Determination of the key criteria

(3) Detailed planning of the constituent parts of the profile

(4) Discussion of the probable implications for the institution resulting from implementation

(5) A programme to prepare potential users

(6) Regular and systematic evaluation and modification

The time-scale for working through this plan will of course vary from place to place but no profiling system is likely to be introduced effectively with less than one year's thorough planning and preparatory work. Curriculum discussions resulting from this preparatory stage may prolong this period. Teachers must have confidence in their own ability to operate the scheme and this can only come from understanding the processes involved and in-service training in appropriate methods of assessment and recording. Teachers are more likely to have confidence in the scheme if they are convinced that the profile has been adapted or designed to

achieve the particular aims of their school or college

provide positive assistance to their own students in the learning process, and

help them teach more effectively.

The preparatory period is thus of crucial importance for the long-term success of the scheme.

Chapter 4

PROFILE PLANNING:
Institutional self-evaluation

During the planning stage two questions essential to effective development have to be answered

(1) Where are we now?

~~**(2)** Where do we wish to go?~~

They can be answered in either order. Answers to question **(2)** will determine the direction of the development; answers to question **(1)** will indicate how much work is involved by highlighting the shortcomings of existing practice.

Self-evaluation is not easy and can appear threatening because it puts professional competence under the microscope. But it must be done before development can take place and everyone concerned should undertake it with mutual trust and respect. Remember that its purpose is to provide an accurate and comprehensive picture of existing assessment and recording practice to facilitate future development.

Four significant areas of school organisation and practice must be evaluated.

The curriculum

Assessment policies

Recording and reporting systems

Pastoral, counselling and guidance systems

Such a review of critical areas of the school structure will undoubtedly also lead to a reappraisal of the aims of the school.

The initial evaluation is meant to provide the basic information needed for creating the key criteria for detailed profile design.

Evaluation does not, however, end at that point. It must continue, both formally and informally, throughout the design and operational stages. The whole process is developmental and therefore requires constant evaluation by the school, the departments and individual teachers.

There are many publications, including an increasing number of local education authority (LEA) evaluation schedules, which can assist in self-evaluation but the process will be illustrated here by considering the assessment policies of the institution which are in practice inevitably closely related to recording and reporting policies.

In his introduction to *In-School Evaluation* Marten Shipman outlines a series of questions arising out of discussions with teachers in London and the Midlands and which shape the format of his book. These are

(1) Are we to assess the attainment of pupils, the efforts they make, their improvement or deterioration or some other attribute?

(2) How much of what goes on in schools is not capable of assessment?

(3) How can we make the assessment of pupils useful to them, to their parents, to their teachers and to their prospective employers?

(4) What information about student performance should be made public?

(5) Given the little time that we have left after teaching in school how can we get the maximum value out of the time we devote to evaluation?

You can easily translate this series into a set of questions which would provide information about current practice in assessment, such as:

Do we currently assess the following in our own students?

> Attainment
> Improvement from term to term
> Lack of improvement from term to term
> Effort
> Other attributes (please indicate)

Assessment must not be considered too narrowly when answering these questions. It should not only be equated with

(1) *End-of-term or end-of-course tests* – it has an important role daily as part of a dynamic teacher/student relationship

(2) *Formal testing* – it has an important role informally, building a picture over time so that assessment can contribute towards a wider range of purposes

(3) *Formal recording* – it has an important role in day-to-day informal judgements which are only recorded when it is thought beneficial and appropriate

So that a comprehensive picture can emerge, questions about the content of assessment will need to be supplemented by questions about *methods, timing* and *the range of students involved.*

Another approach to the problem was suggested by Garforth in his book, *Profile Assessment: Recording Student Progress.* The school or college might randomly select a number of current students and see what information is available about them from the assessment process, how it is presented and what practical use is made of it. Recording student information which is never effectively used is as wasteful of material and human resources as having none. As assessment information is collated, the school or college must consider the main uses for it and the main purposes of the assessment process.

What is assessment used for?

Diagnosis

Evaluation

Guidance

Grading

Selection

Prediction

Why are we assessing? is an essential question but is often not asked. It should be because its answer determines the content, form, method and timing of assessment.

How the evaluation exercise is carried out is largely irrelevant. It is the process that matters and it seems logical for a school or college to use an evaluation schedule available from within its own local education authority. The example below comes from Solihull.

SOLIHULL

Pupil Assessment, Record Keeping and Reporting

(1) Pupil progress is carefully monitored by reliable tests.

(2) There is effective discussion and guidance on the purpose and methods of assessment.

(3) Tests are carefully designed to test objectives set in terms of knowledge, skills and applications which are agreed to be important.

(4) An appropriate variety of tests and evaluation methods are used; standardised achievement tests, diagnostic tests, continuous assessment methods.

(5) Assessment methods are used effectively to diagnose the needs and problems of individual pupils.

(6) Assessment results, when required, are properly standardised to allow proper comparison to be made.

(7) Pupils' work is checked carefully and frequently.

(8) Marking and assessment are used constructively to direct and/or motivate pupils and to improve their performance.

(9) Pupils with particular problems are helped immediately.

(10) Reports are legible, clearly expressed and free from errors.

(11) Reports are full and detailed.

(12) Reports are designed to improve appreciation of pupils' strengths and weaknesses for the benefit of parents and the pupils themselves.

(13) Reports indicate ways of improving performance.

(14) Time is devoted by staff to discussing report writing. Guidance is given.

(15) Record cards are clear, systematic and detailed.

(16) Records of pupil performance and progress are efficiently stored and accessible.

(17) Record cards are kept up-to-date and are accurate and detailed.

(18) The records include details relating to the school objectives.

Chapter 5

PROFILE PLANNING:
Developing the key criteria

There is more likely to be effective design and development if there is an overall plan of development and if the critical characteristics and issues are agreed in advance. Staff will then be working towards common aims understood by all and providing reference points during the design stage. The main issues to be considered are

(1) What are the main purposes of the profile?

(2) Who is to be profiled?

(3) What is to be assessed?

(4) How is the assessment to be undertaken?

(5) Who is to be involved in the assessment process?

(6) How are the results of the assessment to be recorded?

These questions are of course interrelated and the answer to any one of them will have implications for the others. By starting with purpose and ending with recording, the order of the questions is logical.

What kinds of answer might be given to these questions?

1. WHAT ARE THE MAIN PURPOSES OF THE PROFILE?

Profiles are designed to fulfil many different purposes. Practical problems arise when the method of assessment and the recording systems are not related to the main purposes of the assessment. Answers to such questions as, *What is the profile for?*, *Who is to benefit from the exercise?* and *What use will be made of the information?* will determine the design of the profile. Of all the questions relating to profile development, those relating to purpose are the most critical.

To answer these questions, you may find it useful to decide what the purposes of the profile are for various people. For example

People	Possible Purposes
Pupil	Guidance
Teacher	Guidance and evaluation
Head of Department	Evaluation, selection and prediction
Head or Principal	Evaluation
Future teachers	Diagnosis, selection and prediction
Parents	Guidance and prediction
Employers	Selection

It has already been said that a profile will inevitably serve more than one purpose. The balance and emphasis of these purposes must, however, be considered. Should the main focus be *inward* and designed to assist the student by identifying how well someone is learning? Or should the main focus be *outward* and designed to assist some outsider who wants information about what has already been learned by the student?

The purposes outlined in *Records of Achievement: A Statement of Policy* suggest that the profile ought to consist of both a formative recording system and a summative document of record

'The Secretaries of State believe that there are four main purposes which records of achievement and the associated recording systems should serve. These purposes overlap to some extent.
i) Recognition of achievement. Records and recording systems should recognise, acknowledge and give credit for what pupils have achieved and experienced, not just in terms of results in public examinations but in other ways as well. They should do justice to pupils' own efforts and to the efforts of teachers, parents, ratepayers and taxpayers to give them a good education.
ii) Motivation and personal development. They should contribute to pupils' personal development and progress by improving their motivation, providing encouragement and increasing their awareness of strengths, weaknesses and opportunities.

iii) Curriculum and organisation. The recording process should help schools to identify the all round potential of their pupils and to consider how well their curriculum, teaching and organisation enable pupils to develop the general, practical and social skills which are to be recorded.

iv) A document of record. Young people leaving school or college should take with them a short, summary document of record which is recognised and valued by employers and institutions of further and higher education. This should provide a more rounded picture of candidates for jobs or courses than can be provided by a list of examination results, thus helping potential users to decide how candidates could best be employed, or for which jobs, training schemes or courses they are likely to be suitable.'

Records of Achievement: A Statement of Policy
Department of Education and Science, 1984, p. 3

We believe that the main focus of a profile should be formative to assist the student in the learning process and the teacher in evaluating the curriculum. If the focus lies firmly within the classroom it will be possible to extract information for the benefit of a third party. A summative profile which places its emphasis on a third party may well be beneficial for the future of the student, but it cannot effectively assist the learning process because it is concerned with showing what has already been learned rather than improving the quality of learning.

A formative profile will, however, make more demands than a summative one on the structure and organisation of the school and the management of the classroom.

2. WHO IS TO BE PROFILED?

The answer to this question will be largely determined by the answers given to the previous question. There are a number of possible answers.

All the pupils in the year
All students on a specific course
Students ill-served by the external examination system
Students who wish to be involved

The Department of Education and Science (DES) policy statement has largely specified who should be profiled in schools. It makes it clear that the process ought to include every student irrespective of their academic ability or their involvement in external examinations.We agree with this policy because if the process is to be formative and related to the school's learning objectives, then every student must be involved, but contents of the profile will not be the same for every student. The profile will need to be designed to take account of the particular needs of those who, in comparison with others, will achieve little in certain academic areas. If they are to be motivated, the profile will need to record relatively small steps in their progress.

Profiles so far have generally involved students in their final two years of compulsory education. The policy statement indicates that recording systems should be cumulative and begin at the introduction to the secondary phase. This will be of enormous value to the student and to future teachers and other potential users as the student transfers at different points in his or her career to other institutions, courses, or training schemes.

3. WHAT IS TO BE ASSESSED?

If the profile is for employers it need only contain relatively limited information. But if it is to be formative and reflect the curriculum objectives and aims of the course or institution, then it ought to contain details of the full range of both formal and informal learning experiences. *All assessments should be valid and reliable.* Too often profiles contain assessments based on little evidence or generalised statements based on highly specific but limited evidence. Profiles should contain only those areas of learning experiences where there is evidence to make assessments. This is difficult because there is an important difference between assessments based on unavailable evidence and those based on evidence which is available but difficult to assess because the techniques to do so are largely undeveloped. Assessment of important curriculum objectives should not be avoided because the techniques are undeveloped; more appropriate assessment methods should be developed. As Rowntree states in *Assessing Students: How shall we know them?*:

'The important should become assessable, not the assessable important'. Many of the profiling pioneers have experimented with various methods of assessment which might suit the complex range of school and course curriculum objectives.

At this stage in the development programme it is important to identify which broad areas might be included in the profile. These would seem to be

Subject assessments or course objectives
Cross-curricular skills
Personal and social skills
Achievements and experiences

Subject assessments

The existing formal secondary school curriculum is normally seen in terms of subjects. Despite interdisciplinary developments and progress towards a modular curriculum, future profile development is likely to continue concentrating on subjects.

In colleges of further education and Manpower Services Commission schemes specific course components might be identifiable even if these are not always spelt out strictly as subjects.

We see great advantages in recording progress and achievements within subjects or course components. This would lead students to a clearer understanding of their successes in relation to the specific objectives of the subject or course component. It would also encourage a better understanding of the whole curriculum package and the relationship between the objectives of different subjects or course components.

To do this, each department or curriculum area must identify clearly the *skills*, *concepts*, *attitudes* and *knowledge* which students should develop and learn to attain success. This means that the question

'What did I expect the student to learn in the lesson or course?'

will be followed by other related questions such as

'How successful has the student been in mastering those objectives?'

and

'Which objectives have not been mastered and why not?'

The objectives for many students in the upper parts of the secondary school will be related to the national criteria of the GCSE. The profile should be developed so that the assessment criteria for each subject takes account of these national criteria. Indeed, a subject profile in which student progress and achievements are recorded regularly can only assist the teacher in the school-based assessment required for GCSE.

Records of Achievement: A Statement of Policy also states that

'The summary document of record should in principle show pupils' achievements in public examinations including graded results in 16+ and 18+ examinations . . . and the levels of achievement associated with particular grades, such as the national criteria for the General Certificate of Secondary Education (GCSE) and the grade-related criteria for these examinations which are to be developed shortly.'

Cross-curricular skills

In many learning situations some skills have to be mastered before others can be achieved. These prerequisite skills might include

Listening
Measuring
Reading
Writing
Speaking
Numeracy
Manual dexterity
Physical co-ordination

It is important to identify

(1) the extent to which such skills are used throughout the curriculum
(2) the levels of success required, and
(3) the student response to these requirements

because specific weaknesses anywhere will be compounded across different learning situations and will prevent acquisition of the related and dependent skills.

Teachers need to discuss relative strengths and weaknesses of individual students in acquiring and developing such skills in specific learning situations. The inclusion of cross-curricular skills in the profile has implications for the structure and organisation of the institution because time will be required for staff to discuss the performance of individual students in different situations. Such exchanges are invaluable because they lead to a closer understanding of student progress and achievement and to greater insights into curriculum appraisal. Some departments and teachers are too often unaware of other departments' aims and objectives and wrongly assume that certain departments are actively promoting certain key cross-curricular skills. Such dialogues will encourage total curriculum evaluation and the identification of curriculum *overkill* and *underkill*.

Personal and social skills

Developing personal and social skills should be seen as fundamental to the promotion of a broad curriculum and should be included within an institution's core aims. Sometimes the development of personal and social skills should take precedence over the development of specific academic skills.

We would maintain that informal assessments are already regularly made in this area and that there is much to gain from these assessments being discussed with the students since they are a useful means of aiding progress and development.

Assessing personal and social skills is very difficult because the techniques are often inappropriate and the recording methods rarely encourage effective dialogue between the teacher and the student. We use the word *skills* here rather than *qualities* because of the relationship between the development of personal and social skills and the curriculum. The assessment should not constitute a judgement of personality or personal qualities based on a subjective interpretation of an event. *Assessment should be related to specific skills designated as curriculum objectives*, actively promoted within the curriculum and based on discrete evidence. In this way it is identified with a specific performance and is not capable of generalisation.

The promotion of personal and social skills has been given fresh impetus in further education and in schemes initiated by the Manpower Services Commission (MSC). They are regarded as core components in courses developed within the TVEI and as part of the CPVE. Skills of communication, problem-solving and decision-making are likely to be essential for surviving in a rapidly changing world.

As with cross-curricular skills, the inclusion of personal and social skills has clear implications for the structure and organisation of the institution. They must be identifiable within the curriculum, and time must be made available for teachers to discuss student performance in different situations, with each other and with the student.

Achievements and experiences

Education can no longer only be thought of as a structured process occurring in a classroom during school hours. Some of the most meaningful learning experiences can occur outside the classroom either in extra-curricular or out-of-school activities. A school or college can benefit a lot from knowing what a student has achieved and experienced in this way and may be able to relate it to the objectives of the structured curriculum. Some experiences can only be recorded and not assessed in any formal way, but any record of achievement would be incomplete without full reference to a wide range of curricular and extra-curricular achievements and experiences.

We believe that the range of assessments in the profile and record of achievement must be broad enough to reflect the students' learning experiences from the many declared objectives of the institution. For this reason the profile ought to contain each of the four components identified.

4. HOW IS THE ASSESSMENT TO BE UNDERTAKEN?

This question will be considered in more detail later but it is important to decide at the planning stage what kind of comparison is to be made in assessment. Each student can be compared against

fellow students,
specified learning objectives, and
his or her own past performance and/or potential.

The most common kind of comparison currently used is student against student. It is interested in a competitive level of performance which is usually expressed in grades. If the profile is to help students to learn, this emphasis must change. Performance must be related to expectation.

This produces clear implications for the individual teacher, department and institution. Each teacher will need to

(1) have a much sharper definition of what skills, knowledge and understanding should be developed in each course component, and
(2) establish clear criteria for assessment based on these learning objectives .

Relating curriculum and assessment objectives in this way enables assessment to become an aid to learning rather than a repetitive constraint.

There is no reason why discussions between teacher and student should not also relate performance to the student's own past record and/or potential. This can help the student understand the often difficult concept of progress more clearly. It is even better if such discussions produce agreement on some clear short-term and long-term goals for the future.

5. WHO IS TO BE INVOLVED IN THE ASSESSMENT PROCESS?

Most assessment is currently carried out by teachers. It concentrates on the individual student in a specific situation and is usually related to limited objectives. If assessment becomes broader by including, for example, cross-curricular skills and personal and social skills, then it is essential to include in the assessment every teacher involved with the student. Assessment designed principally to assist student learning must also involve the students fully.

The inclusion of achievements and experiences from outside the formal curriculum are likely to involve assessments made by outsiders such as the employer responsible for Work Experience or the leader of the Duke of Edinburgh Award scheme. The institution should identify what problems will result from including such assessments which involve both *judgement of student achievement* and *ratification of student experience.*

We believe that including a wide range of people in the assessment process is very useful: it gives a wider perspective to student achievements and experiences and involves the committed parties in a practical way in the whole educational process.

6. HOW ARE THE RESULTS OF THE ASSESSMENT TO BE RECORDED?

The recording methods currently used are extremely restricted and rarely comprise more than grades, marks and, perhaps, a short written comment. This fails to reveal a lot of useful information and can even mask the truth. The student not only wishes to receive a general opinion on a specific piece of work or course but also needs to know specific strengths and weaknesses and to receive precise advice regarding appropriate action. So there is a need to move towards systems of recording which provide such details and relate achievement to specific objectives which are clearly understood by all concerned.

'Good examples always linked closely carefully planned work and some form of assessment. In these examples the record was an essential tool for the teacher in planning the next stage. For a record to be of use, it has to comment upon the effectiveness of what has been done and contain information vital to the teacher's understanding of the pupil's learning problems.'

Slow learning and less successful pupils in secondary schools
HMI Report, 1984

Chapter 6 will contain examples of recording systems designed to provide such detailed information in a variety of situations.

Before detailed planning can take place in any school or college, broad general agreement must be reached on the answers given to the six critical questions posed in this chapter. Those answers may, quite rightly, differ from our views.

PROFILE PLANNING:
Detailed planning of the constituent parts

We have already said that assessment must reflect the curriculum objectives of the department and the institution. The profile must therefore result from detailed staff discussion about what students should learn. This then naturally leads to questions such as

What should be assessed?

How do individual students respond to assessment and curriculum objectives?

How should these responses be recorded?

It is very difficult for busy teachers to start discussing such things from scratch so it might be helpful to study other examples and ideas to provoke discussion and further thought. Remember that each example will have been designed for a specific context and will therefore probably need to be modified to fulfil your needs exactly.

For each of the possible profile components suggested in Chapter 5, namely

Subject assessment
Cross-curricular skills
Personal and social skills
Achievements and experiences

the following three questions will be asked and a number of possible answers suggested:

(1) What are the criteria for assessment?

(2) What is the most appropriate method of assessment for each of the chosen criteria?

(3) How is the information to be recorded?

SUBJECT ASSESSMENT

What are the criteria for assessment?

Most teachers attempt to develop many objectives for any course and it is impossible to assess everything. The department or course team must therefore *identify those criteria which are critical as a basis for assessment and recording* because they are vital for helping the student to learn and the teacher to evaluate the teaching.

Curriculum and assessment criteria can be expressed in several ways so that both student and teacher might be led to a critical evaluation of their own learning and teaching. These are

    Course content
    Unit outcomes
    Teaching goals
    Process skills

Course Content

By expressing the criteria in terms of course content, student performance can be related to the whole course or to specific parts of the course.

An example of this is seen on the following Subject Tutor Report for Geography from Norton Priory School, Runcorn, shown on page 33.

Unit Outcomes

There has been a trend in recent years for courses to be based on units or modules and to create short, self-contained modules lasting, say, six weeks. The Subject Tutor Report for Geography could be redesigned to provide information about the student in relation to a part of the course, such as the weather and climate in Britain.

It is likely that there will be further development work on courses based on modules or units. Student motivation can obviously benefit from courses being divided into shorter modules. These can provide students with short-term goals which can be easily identified and which provide manageable and achieveable learning tasks. Many existing courses lend themselves readily to such treatment.

SUBJECT TUTOR REPORT

GEOGRAPHY

JOINT GCE 'O' LEVEL AND C.S.E

The aim of this course is for
pupils to develop an understanding of the relationships
between man and his natural
and man-made environment. These
interrelationships are considered
at a variety of scales ranging
from the study of small areas to
the study of the world as a whole.

The subject content is divided
into 3 areas.

1. Selected World Studies
2. England, Wales and Scotland
3. Studies in Northern England

Each area is studied in relation
to the main features of its
population, relief, climate,
agriculture, power resources,
distribution of industry,
settlement, transport networks
and leisure facilities.

The work is tested by two examination
papers:

Paper 1 (35%) consists of objective
questions drawn from the whole syllabus.
Paper 2 (40%) consists of structured
questions including those of the essay
type as well as data response questions.
Again questions are drawn from the whole
syllabus.

An assessment of fieldwork makes
up the final 25% of the examination
mark. This requires the submission of
a major fieldwork folder by each pupil.
The folder should consist of a first
hand investigation carried out in the
local environment.

NAME OF
PUPIL:- . . . .

FORM:- . . . .

LEVEL OF ACHIEVEMENT:-

      'O' LEVEL
      C.S.E.

ANTICIPATED FINAL EXAMINATION GRADE:-

     . . . .

SUBJECT TUTOR'S COMMENTS.

SIGNED:- . . . .

DATE:- . . . .

Modules are also being developed by other agencies such as examination boards. The list of unit outcomes from the record of achievement for the West Midlands Examinations Board (see below) states explicitly what must be attained before a certificate can be awarded for that unit.

Students also need longer-term objectives and modules must be carefully selected if the proper breadth and balance of curricular objectives are to be achieved and if specific student needs are to be met.

The West Midlands Examinations Board

Record of Achievement

LIST OF UNIT OUTCOMES

Scheme Title: Mathematics

Reference: WAR/MA/1
Number of units in scheme: 10

Unit Reference	Unit Title	Unit Stage
MA2	Mathematics	2

Unit Outcomes:

Knowledge

The student can:

1. distinguish between income and expenditure.
2. explain how accounts are used in commercial organisations.
3. explain the reasons for supporting account entries with credit and debit vouchers.
4. prepare two alternative forms of account sheet.
5. explain the basic principles and reasons for audit of accounts.

Skills

The student can:

6. complete a range of forms and statements which relate to the personal financial affairs of a young adult.
7. maintain a simple account sheet.
8. maintain credit and debit vouchers in relation to an account.
9. balance and audit a simple account.
10. use the basic rules of arithmetic as they relate to money.
11. estimate simple money calculations mentally.
12. use a calculator to undertake elementary calculations relating to personal finance.
13. explain three of the charges which are made by banks for maintaining a personal account.

Experiences

The student has:

14. maintained an account in a simulated commercial environment.
15. visited a bank and experienced the daily routine of a bank counter clerk.
16. handled and completed a range of forms and statements relating to the personal finances of a young adult.

The West Midlands Examinations Board

Record of Achievement

STAGE CERTIFICATE

Roger A Jones

This certificate certifies that .... has successfully achieved the outcomes of the following unit course.

Unit Reference **MA2**	Unit Title **Mathematics**	Unit Stage **2**
M W Corke		*B. Swift*
M W Corke Chairman	Date of Award ....10th May 1985	B Swift Secretary

---

Teaching Goals

Identifying what is to be learned from any course is a useful first stage in the assessment process. The more precise this identification is, the easier the assessment usually becomes.

Specified goals can be clearly identified as *general goals* which *all students* should aim to achieve. Specific goals may also be related to *particular ranges of ability* or for *individual students*. The advantages of such an approach are clear.

(1) The student is aware of the particular learning objectives of the course or subject and the assessment can identify achievements and areas of difficulty quite precisely.

(2) The teacher gets some useful information about what the curriculum needs of the individual and the whole group are.

If many students fail to achieve particular objectives this will suggest the need for some broad remedial action and will provide evidence on which to base that action.

The following examples show how goals may be identified for whole groups, specific ability ranges and individual students.

Group goals

In the example shown opposite taken from the Designing, Planning and Implementation section of the Assessment of Performance Unit (APU) document, *Design and Technology*, a series of teaching

TABLE I

DESIGNING, PLANNING AND IMPLEMENTATION

1. DESIGNING

1.1 FIT

1.1.1 Can a child perceive (describe, discuss or otherwise communicate) or identify through investigation a fit or misfit between an artefact or system and set of human requirements (desires, needs)?

1.1.2 Can a child judge the quality of the fit or misfit ('How well does it work?') and express this judgement?

1.1.3 Can a child recognise that something might be done to improve, rectify or change an artefact, or if there is a good fit, to leave things as they are?

1.1.4 Can a child identify criteria which are relevant to improving the quality of fit?

1.2 HOLISM

1.2.1 Can a child analyse a misfit ('Design problem') in such a way that he takes into account such factors and considerations as:
i.   Economic (cost, time, availability of materials).

ii. Social (awareness of others and of the effect of the designed artefact/system upon them).

iii. Ethical (morality of proposed change).

1.2.2 Can a child mould all the aspects of a design problem in a balanced, interactive way

1.2.3 Can a child fit ends to means as well as means to ends?

1.3 FORMULATION

1.3.1 Can a child state or restate the design problem? (In order to arrive at its essence.)

1.3.2 Can a child look at a particular solution and work backwards to reformulate the original problem?

1.3.3 Can a child generate a variety of possible provisions (solutions) to a design problem?

1.4 CONVERGENCY

1.4.1 Can a child decrease the variety of possible solutions and show commitment to a specific, practical proposal?

1.4.2 Can a child explain and justify the reason for his choice of one in preference to others?

1.5 DATA SEARCH

1.5.1 Can a child recognise the need for the collection of information which is appropriate to the problem?

1.5.2 Can a child search for, generate, collate and judge the reliability and usefulness of information?

1.5.3 Can a child apply the relevant information, which he has obtained, to aid the solution of the problem?

1.6 IMAGING OR COGNITIVE MODELLING

1.6.1 Can the child conjure up a description of an artefact, system (or parts of such things) in the mind's eye?

1.6.2 Can he manipulate the images? (Rotate, assemble, change colour or texture, cause interpenetration or change form.)

1.6.3 Can the child express these images? (Sketch, model, etc.)

1.7 DESIGN MODELLING

1.7.1 Can a child demonstrate the purpose of modelling ? (Iconic, symbolic, analogue.)

a. to simplify (by reduction to essentials)
b. to show correspondence (eg by analogy)
c. to give emphasis (eg to salient features)
d. to extrapolate (eg trends)
e. to simulate (eg lighting change)

1.7.2 Can a child detect the limit of usefulness of a form of modelling ? (eg when scaling down invalidates a model)

1.7.3 Can a child translate one form of model or simulation to another form or to reality ? (eg circuit diagram to assembled components)

2. PLANNING, IMPLEMENTATION AND EVALUATION

2.1 PLANNING

2.1.1 Can a child cost the production of an artefact or system? (In terms of use of materials resources, time, energy, social effects.)

2.1.2 Can a child distinguish between the difference of producing a single artefact or manufacturing for bulk production?

2.1.3 Can a child plan a sequence of operations in an appropriate order which will lead to the production of an artefact or system?

2.2 IMPLEMENTATION

2.2.1 Can a child demonstrate that he is alert to the possibility that an unforeseen difficulty may arise during making which may indicate an alternative means of realisation or production?

2.2.2 Can a child deal effectively with such difficulties by acquiring new strategies, information or skills?

2.2.3 Can a child execute a task with due regard to the need for safe practice?

2.2.4 Can a child choose and use appropriate tools, materials and appliances to achieve his purpose?

2.3 EVALUATION

2.3.1 Can a child evaluate and offer a continuing critique on the process and progress of his design?

2.3.2 Can a child re-evaluate at the conclusion of realisation (after a suitable interval of time) the quality of the match between design and need?

2.3.3 Can a child analyse and evaluate the approach and solution adopted by other designers?

goals is proposed to underline any activity undertaken in this area. The list acts as a template across any detailed curriculum provision. Teachers may find this idea useful and it is being developed in several curriculum areas within different schemes. It has the advantage of providing a structure for both the assessment and the curriculum planning.

Ability ranges goals

The example (opposite) of language learning goals taken from the Appendix to the HMI document *Curriculum 11–16: Towards a Statement of Entitlement* attempts to differentiate learning goals for broad bands of ability.

If assessment is to assist the student in the learning process then it must be related to attainable goals. A department may need to examine critically what students should learn so it can identify those goals which should be achieved by all students and those which will only be achieved by some students. The only way to do this successfully is to set individual learning goals for each student, which many teachers do in the way described in the following flowchart.

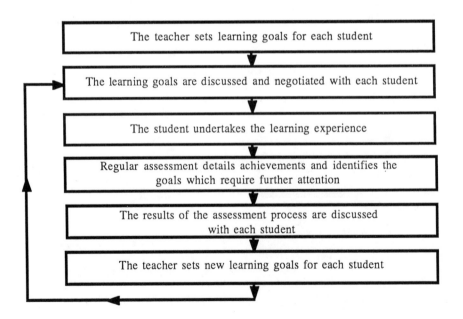

Appendix

The following table outlines a range of possible language learning goals, on the one hand for pupils who are likely to cease their study of a foreign language after 2 or 3 years and, on the other, for those who continue their study at least until age 16; mid-course goals are also suggested for those pupils who intend to pursue their study beyond the third year. The relevance of these goals to the groups indicated will depend on local factors.

	Goals for pupils likely to terminate their study after		Goals after 3 years of study for abler pupils likely to complete a 5 year course	Goals for those completing a 5 year course	
	3 years	3, 4 or 5 years depending on local circumstances and on motivation		Able pupils	Very able pupils
Listening	Understanding of concrete everyday language used in specified situations; ability to identify subject matter of speech so as to respond in English or by action. Understanding of concrete language within wider range of lexis and structures.	Understanding of everyday language in an increasing range of situations.	Greater understanding of everyday language spoken at near normal speed.	Detailed understanding of concrete language spoken by a native at near normal speed and involving familiar language already; gist understanding of language similarly spoken over wider range of lexis structures.	Detailed understanding of language spoken by a native at near normal speed within areas of language already encountered but including abstract forms: gist understanding of language containing some unfamiliar lexis.
Reading	Recognition reading of a simple routine nature: shop signs, labels, products, signs etc. Wider range of vocabulary and structures: gist reading of a more consecutive nature.	Understanding of simple items such as letters, notices and short narrative texts.	Detailed reading of items such as letters, notices and simple foreign texts; gist understanding of a wider range of reading material.	Detailed and gist understanding of concrete language in newspapers, advertisements, formal and informal letters and possibly adapted foreign texts.	Detailed and gist understanding of fiction and of non-fiction studied intensively or extensively.
Speaking	Two-language communication with each speaker using his own language. The ability to ask for simple information in the foreign language; further speech in English.	The ability to ask and answer specified questions satisfying simple routine needs and minimum courtesy requirements.	The ability to ask and answer questions concerning everyday needs and including simple narrative and description (in tenses other than the present).	The ability to ask and answer questions in a wider variety of situations and involving increasing complexity of structure and breadth of vocabulary.	Relatively fluent, flexible and accurate use of language: some measure of confidence in initiating language and in expressing interests, feelings and ideas.
Writing	Of no significance as a goal but practised as an aid to memorisation and to teacher serenity.	Reproduction of language encountered in speech (above); very simple letter-writing.	Writing of dialogue, narrative and simple letters of a personal type.	Personal writing about family, home and interests; letters and simple compositions.	Relatively accurate and fluent personal writing about family, home and interests as well as narrative and descriptive composition.
	Least able pupils	Below average pupils	Pupils of average ability	Able pupils	Very able pupils

NAME: Marta

SUBJECT: English   YEAR LEVEL: 8   TERM: II

	Yes	No
1 COMPLETE PROJECT/PERSONAL PROJECT		
Project was 7 pages, well set out, clear headings and interesting photographs. The story about grandfather explained very well what his work used to be like and how your work, when you leave school, will be very different.		
2 READ NOVEL 'SUPERFUDGE' AND COMPLETE ASSIGNMENT		
All the work was completed but next time consider taking more time thinking about the answers. Your written answers shouldn't tell the story again but be about what you believe the story is telling us.		
3 COMPLETE REGULAR SPELLING, COMPREHENSION AND VOCABULARY WORK		
Completed and corrected.		
4 WRITE 3 STORIES AND WORK ON IMPROVING THEM		
All stories were improved by re-writng and you should be very pleased. Your story 'Survival' was exciting to read. You could use it for reading to the Grade 5 pupils next term.		
5 KEEP A JOURNAL AND WRITE IN IT EVERY DAY		
You seem to enjoy writing in your journal. You might like to copy out 2 poems for the wall display.		
6 CO-OPERATE WITH TEACHER AND OTHER STUDENTS, PARTICIPATE IN CLASS ACTIVITIES AND BRING NECESSARY MATERIALS TO CLASS		
This term has been important for you in that you often spoke in class discussions and helped organise our excursion. You must remember to complete all work on time. Next term use your diary entries as reminders.		

SUMMARY: For Parents

- All assessment goals for Term II English have been completed.
- Marta improved her writing this term because she carefully followed instructions, and worked quietly in class.
- She has been a little late with some work and next term should use her diary. If the tasks are hard she should tell me.
- I look forward to discussing Marta's work with you at the parent-teacher meeting.

Individual student goals

The example on page 39, facing, is taken from work on English profiling by the Victorian Institute of Secondary Education (VISE), Melbourne, Australia; it relates individual student performance to six specific teaching goals. It is possible to interpret many of these goals as belonging to the individual student, although there is no direct evidence that this is so. It is also interesting that the parents are drawn into this assessment process in a very positive way.

Process Skills

A further approach in identifying criteria for assessment is to concentrate not on the teaching goals but on the means or process by which the student arrives at these goals. The assessment objectives can be related to the process skills required either to complete successfully different modules or areas of content or to achieve specific teaching goals. The Inner London Education Authority (ILEA)/Further and Higher Education (FHE) Curriculum Development Project Science Skills Checklist Record Sheet shown overleaf identifies two broad sets of process skills, considered necessary for developing a scientific approach to problems. These skills are 'Observing/Measuring' and 'Planning Problem-Solving' which are claimed to be used in all scientific experiments and explorations. (This development has now been integrated with the RSA Process Skills Profile.)

The research and development work supporting the promotion of the Oxford Certificate of Educational Achievement (OCEA) has also proposed process skills as the most meaningful way to consider progressive assessment in subjects such as mathematics and science or in the perception of certain features as in English and modern languages. These process skills proposals are illustrated on pages 42 and 43.

Student _____   Tutor _____   ILEA © 1982

Task & dates Skills									
S1 Observing/Measuring				**S2.8** Practising Health and Safety procedures			
S1.1 Observing				**S2.9** Working systematically (a) following instructions (b) following own plan			
S1.2 Classifying							
S1.3 Using representational diagrams/symbols				**S2.10** Working effectively (a) work individually to complete a task (b) co-operate to complete a task			
S1.4 Selecting/using appropriate measuring devices							
S1.5 Estimating/approximating				**S2.11** Using computer assisted methods			
S1.6 (i) Measuring (ii) Calculating/using measurement of scientific units				**S2.12** Maintaining tools/equipment/living things			
				S2.13 Planning investigations using suitable (i) living/non-living material (ii) tools, equipment			
S2 Planning Problem-Solving							
S2.1 Identifying a problem							
S2.2 Suggesting explanations, causes, solutions				**S2.14** Designing an investigation/using idea of a control			
S2.3 Selecting likely explanations, causes, solutions				**S2.15** Assembling components for an investigation			
S2.4 Testing likely explanations, causes, solutions				**S2.16** Recording (i) procedure (ii) relevant observations			
S2.5 Examining critically				**S2.17** Drawing conclusions at an appropriate stage			
S2.6 Devising/using models							
S2.7 Implementing solutions and monitoring outcomes				**S2.18** Evaluating (i) investigation (ii) own performance			

MATHEMATICS

PROCESSES

INTERPRETING

ORGANISING

MEASURING

CALCULATING

REPRESENTING
CHECKING/EVALUATING

EXPLAINING/JUSTIFYING

CONJECTURING/
GENERALISING

ENTRY

ATTACK

RESOLUTION

Interpreting and understanding
the problem: What is it about ?
What has to be done ?
Organising and planning the
approach: determining the overall
strategy and tactics to be adopted.

Applying the tactics: using the
skills that are needed in the
overall strategy.

Finding the possible outcomes
and checking that they are
appropriate. Keeping the strategy
in mind and reviewing the tactics
to ensure good/successful/
reasonable outcomes.

Presenting findings with
reasons/evidence and with
suggestions for further
development and ways forward.

SCIENCE

Planning

Performing

Interpreting

Communicating

Formulating problems
Experimental design

Observing
Manipulating
Data gathering

Data handling
Drawing conclusions
Predicting

Reporting
Receiving information

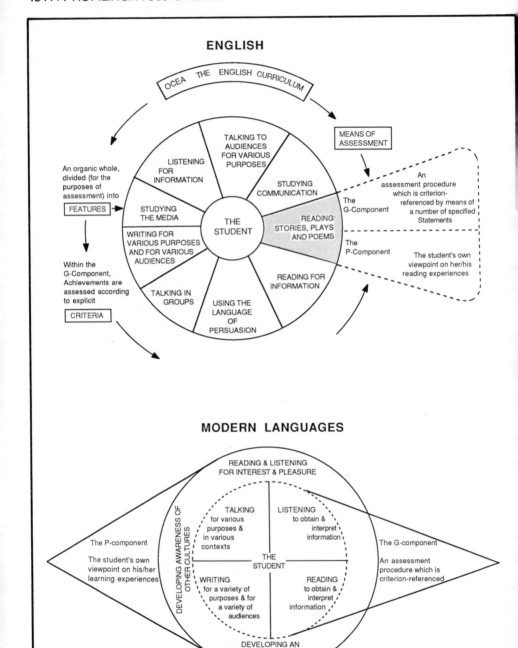

ENGLISH

OCEA THE ENGLISH CURRICULUM

An organic whole, divided (for the purposes of assessment) into

FEATURES

Within the G-Component, Achievements are assessed according to explicit

CRITERIA

LISTENING FOR INFORMATION

TALKING TO AUDIENCES FOR VARIOUS PURPOSES

STUDYING COMMUNICATION

STUDYING THE MEDIA

THE STUDENT

READING STORIES, PLAYS AND POEMS

WRITING FOR VARIOUS PURPOSES AND FOR VARIOUS AUDIENCES

TALKING IN GROUPS

USING THE LANGUAGE OF PERSUASION

READING FOR INFORMATION

MEANS OF ASSESSMENT

The G-Component

An assessment procedure which is criterion-referenced by means of a number of specified Statements

The P-Component

The student's own viewpoint on her/his reading experiences

MODERN LANGUAGES

READING & LISTENING FOR INTEREST & PLEASURE

DEVELOPING AWARENESS OF OTHER CULTURES

TALKING for various purposes & in various contexts

LISTENING to obtain & interpret information

THE STUDENT

WRITING for a variety of purposes & for a variety of audiences

READING to obtain & interpret information

The P-component

The student's own viewpoint on his/her learning experiences

The G-component

An assessment procedure which is criterion-referenced

DEVELOPING AN AWARENESS OF LANGUAGE

What is the most appropriate method of assessment for each of the chosen criteria?

Having selected the criteria for assessment, you must next decide on the most appropriate way of assessing each of them. You will find further help on this in Chapter 7, but you will already realise that relating assessment objectives to curriculum objectives is likely to lead to a shift from comparing student against student towards comparing performance against specified objectives – that is, measuring achievement against expectation. You may also realise that this kind of assessment is more likely to be used for diagnostic purposes and so help the student in the learning process. Broadening the scope of assessment is also likely to mean more use of informal assessment by observation.

Deciding which technique to choose for any criteria is quite complex. The following questions are likely to help you make an appropriate decision.

(1) Does the technique fit the purpose of the assessment?

(2) Does the technique provide the information I am looking for?

(3) Do I fully understand the technique?

(4) Does the student understand the technique?

(5) Do I need to make any special arrangements if I use this technique?

(6) Is it the easiest technique for this criteria? Is it time-efficient?

(7) If I use this technique what form will the evidence take?

Question 7 is critical. Teacher and student both need to be clear about what the student will have to do to demonstrate that learning has actually taken place. Very often in the secondary school classroom there is a very restricted view of what constitutes acceptable or appropriate evidence of learning and student achievement. There should be a more flexible attitude about evidence so that it need not be limited to being expressed in its traditional written form. The checklist overleaf may indicate the range of acceptable and possibly valid forms of evidence.

EVIDENCE FOR ASSESSMENT

Written

Report
Diary/Log
Essay
Story
Questionnaire
Letter
Notes/Draft
Newspaper
Magazine
Storyboard
Display

Visual

Picture
Poster
Film
Video
Photograph
Decoration
Graph/Chart
Printout

3-D

Models
Sculpture
Produce
Artefacts

Oral

Performance
Role-play
Recorded discussions
Recorded conversation
Interview
Debate
Radio programme

How is the information to be recorded?

The most appropriate method of recording the information revealed in assessment then needs to be decided.

An important issue is whether or not to establish a common recording format for use throughout the institution. There are three obvious advantages in creating such a format.

All users will be able to understand the recording system easily.

The students will gain confidence from familiarity with a single system.

It will be easier for teachers with responsibilities for individual students to interpret progress across the full range of learning experiences.

The method selected must be compatible with departmental aims, curriculum objectives and teaching methods. It is likely, however, that the specific needs of individual teachers or departments for particular components of the course will make such a common format difficult to achieve. There is little to gain from insisting on a common format if individual departments believe that the chosen method fails to serve their needs. It may therefore be preferable for each department to develop a method of recording to suit its own needs and those of its students.

The method selected must be convenient and aid, not constrain, the classroom learning process.

The method selected must highlight the information required as simply as possible. There is little point in discovering information which will not be used or in recording it in a form too complex to interpret readily and easily. Above all, *the selected method must stimulate discussion between teacher and student,* to encourage the student to use the resulting information and stimulate progress. This is the most important part of the assessment process and one which is often ignored to the detriment of all concerned. *The method selected must therefore be capable of interpretation by all students.*

The selection of the most appropriate method of recording is a complex task dependent on many factors. There is little point in agreeing on criteria for assessment if selecting an inappropriate method of recording makes it difficult to use the information which the student and teacher require.

There are a number of recording methods currently being developed and evaluated by various institutions and organisations. They include

Grading systems
Progress grids
Checklists
Descriptive assessments
Self-assessments

Grading Systems

The use of grades, particularly in public examinations and school reports, is a firmly established and familiar system which teachers are confident about using.

Unless clear criteria are established as the basis for which grades are awarded, they are subjective and uninformative. The criteria can be either statistical or descriptive. *Statistical grades* are unlikely to encourage feedback or motivation. *Descriptive grades* are much more sensibly used as descriptions rather than as grades themselves.

The use of grades can, however, be useful in the early stages of profile development and may stimulate the design of criteria for assessment by forcing teachers to ask questions such as

'What standards of performance do we seek in order that we might award an A or a B, etc.?'
or
'What evidence do we need from the students to award a particular grade?'

A system which awards grades in French of

Listening	B
Writing	B
Reading	B
Speaking	D

provides more information than an overall grade C and creates a basis for further progress. The example of the Interim Assessment in English Language CSE from Helston School shown opposite illustrates both the problem and the potential.

Progress Grids

Awarding grades according to clear criteria leads naturally to the development of the progress grid where descriptors take the place of grades. They indicate more precisely different levels of achievement for specific skills or goals. This is better than the use of grades alone because clear information is provided for both teacher and

HELSTON SCHOOL PROFILE: FINAL ASSESSMENT

ENGLISH LANGUAGE

COURSE O Level ☐

CSE ☐

Assessment period September 1985 to March 1986

Name .... Tutor Group ....

	A	B	C	D	E
Understanding					
Originality					
Creativity					
Coherence					
Clarity					
Organisational ability					
Fluency					
Mechanical accuracy					
Attitude					

[Grade C is average for the whole age group]

TEACHER'S COMMENTS

Mock Examination Result............................

Signature.......................... Date..........................

student and does not need interpreting. It also enables progress to be portrayed over a period of time.

In practice, however, appropriate descriptors are extremely difficult to create and the use of progress grids might be more appropriate for some departments than others such as English, where difficulties have been experienced.

The examples of progress grids given on pages 49–51 is taken from the assessment of science skills at Pilgrim School, Bedford.

PILGRIM SCHOOL, BEDFORD

SCIENCE:

Name —————————

Period of Assessment —————————

Level of Study —————————

SKILL AREAS			LEVEL 1	LEVEL 2	LEVEL 3	LEVEL 4
SYMBOLS		Graphs, tables charts				
		Scientific symbols. Drawings				
APPARATUS		Measuring instruments and Units				
		Estimating quantities				
		Following instructions				
		Manual dexterity				
OBSERVATION/ INTERPRETATION		Use of keys for identification				
		Comparisons. Data into patterns				
		Generalisations				
		Applying scientific concepts				

SOCIAL	Criticising procedures: practical problem-solving		
	Contribution to small-group activity		
	Usual role in group		

LEVELS DEFINED

Graphs, Tables, Charts
1) Construct suitable tables of data, e.g. experimental results.
2) Read information from tables of data under direction and construct a simple graph under direction.
3) Construct a graph of data without direction and interpolate.
4) Construct a graph, extrapolate, interpolate and explain the kind of relationship shown.

Symbols, Drawings, Scientific notation
1) Identify objects from diagrams.
2) Use/Interpret a diagram to set up apparatus.
3) Make a conventional sectional drawing of apparatus; label common apparatus.
4) Realise real ideas expressed as symbols, e.g. formulae, circuit components.

Measuring Instruments and Units
1) Read a simple scale without subdivisions (with units).
2) Read a simple scale with subdivisions (with units).
3) Read and interpolate on a scale (with units).
4) Select an appropriate range of scale on a multi-scale instrument (with units).

Estimating quantities
1) Estimate simple dimensions of objects.
2) Estimate areas, mass, volume.
3) Estimate more complex/ abstract quantities, e.g. work, power.
4) Estimate the outcome of a calculation involving real quantities.

Following Instructions
1) Set up apparatus or act on simple one-step instructions.
2) Set up apparatus or act on diagrammatic instructions.
3) Follow multi-step but explicit instructions
4) Follow instructions, recalling and using standard procedures to complete a specific task.

Manual dexterity
1) Carry, lift and set down apparatus as directed.
2) Reliably perform basic manipulative tasks.
3) Perform tasks requiring two-handed coordination.
4) Perform tasks requiring high manipulative control of apparatus. e.g. dissection, titration, soldering.

Use of Keys
1) Identify objects by direct comparison.
2) Identify different objects using a branched key.
3) Identify and distinguish similar objects using a branched key.
4) Construct a branched key for identifications.

Comparisons, Data into Patterns
1) Sort objects into groups.
2) List similarities and differences between objects or events.
3) Describe patterns in data or observations.
4) Use patterns to predict further data/results.

Generalisations
1) Identify data which do not fit into a given pattern.
2) Suggest an explanation to fit data; relate a pattern of information to hypothesis.
3) Assess a model as the generalisation of a pattern.
4) Assess the extent to which a generalisation can be applied to a situation.

Applying scientific concepts *(including some recall)*
1) Describe a pattern based on accepted ideas.
2) Make predictions based on information and ideas.
3) Predict from hypothesis or model.
4) Generate hypothesis/model consistent with concepts.

Criticising procedures: Practical problem-solving
1) Identify testable statements; rephrase general statements in a testable form.
2) Select variables to be controlled during procedures.
3) Produce a sensible sequence of steps in a procedure.
4) Suggest a procedure for a simple investigation to solve a problem.

Social Interactions: contribution to small-group activity
1) Passively allows others to perform experiments.
2) Makes little contribution to small-group activity.
3) Makes little contribution to the success of the investigation equal with that of the other members of the group.
4) Makes large contribution to small-group activity. The contribution may be as leader/director, performer, recorder, or the pupil may be an isolate.

Personal Assessment

Name _____ Form _____

Reference will be made to some or all of the following as appropriate: Punctuality Attendance Behaviour Care with appearance Relations with peers Perseverance Effort Interest Responsibility General Attitude Homework	December, 198	
	June, 198	
	January, 198	

General Comment	December, 198	Overall Grade in terms of O Level/C.S.E:

General Comment	June, 198	Overall Grade in terms of O Level/C.S.E:

General Comment	January, 198	Overall Grade in terms of O Level/C.S.E:

FINAL SUMMARY

Teacher _____

SYLLABUS

Examination Grades : G.C.E. O Level : A B C D E
C.S.E.   :   1 2 3 4 5

There is no necessary comparison between the levels of skill performance described on the front page and examination grades.

Checklists

Where specific teaching goals have been identified a checklist method of recording student progress and achievements can be designed. A checklist has several advantages.

(1) It is easy to operate – it is simply ticked when the appropriate skill has been mastered or an objective has been achieved.

(2) It allows a close relationship between the curriculum and assessment objectives and makes curriculum evaluation easy.

(3) It readily identifies student strengths and weaknesses particularly where skills or objectives are grouped broadly and the skills are arranged hierarchically. Broad areas of concern or strengths can be highlighted or specific skills pinpointed for future attention.

But checklists can cause problems if the objectives are not precisely defined. If the descriptions used are too broad, they are difficult to assess and to use validly and effectively. If the descriptions are too narrow, they will create an unmanageable number of criteria.

LENGTH	AREA	VOLUME/CAPACITY
Comparing lengths of objects: vocabulary – "longer", "taller", etc. ☐	Idea of a surface: covering surfaces with paint, sticky paper, etc. ☐	Filling vessels with water, sand, marbles, etc. ☐
Ordering objects by length: vocabulary – "longest", "tallest", etc. ☐	Comparing and ordering areas of regular and irregular shapes by superimposition ☐	Comparing and ordering containers by capacity: vocabulary – "holds more/most", etc. ☐
Use of arbitrary and personal units ☐	Use of arbitrary units ☐	Use of arbitrary units ☐
Conservation of length ☐	Use of unit squares ☐	
Use of standard units: m and cm ☐	Conservation of area ☐	Conservation of volume ☐
Practical estimating and measuring using a variety of instruments ☐	Practical estimating and measuring using grids or standard unit squares (i) using cm^2 ☐ (ii) using m^2 ☐	Practical estimating and measuring of capacity using vessels graduated in: (i) litres/simple fractions of a litre ☐ (ii) cm^3 ☐
Decimal recording (e.g. 3m 62cm = 3.62m) ☐ Use of km ☐ Use of mm ☐	Formulae for areas of: (i) rectangle (incl. square) ☐	
Relationships among units (km/m/cm/mm) ☐	(ii) triangle ☐	Relationship between cm^3 and litre (1 litre = 1000 cm^3) ☐
Further practical activities involving selection of appropriate instruments and units ☐	(iii) circle ☐	
Distance/time/speed problems ☐	Problems involving larger units; (i) km^2 ☐ (ii) are/hectare ☐	Finding volumes of solids by displacement ☐
Simple scale drawing: enlargement/reduction ☐	Scale: how area increases relative to linear scale ☐	Formulae for volume of cube and cuboid ☐

A checklist shows what the student can do although sometimes it is important to record not only the achievement itself but also the quality of it. In Physical Education, for example, providing detail of the style of the stroke in swimming might be as important as recording 'Can swim 25 metres'.

The checklist approach has been widely used in Mathematics and can be found in many primary school record cards or primary/ secondary transfer documents such as the example of the record card on length, area and volume/capacity shown on page 52, and the form, shown below, taken from development work in ILEA to provide a checklist for science skills in secondary schools and colleges of further education.

	S	PROCESS/SKILLS	(PROFILE SENTENCES): "The student is able to . . ."
FAMILY—OBSERVATION	1	Observing as fully as is appropriate	determine the relevant information for a particular situation/enquiry.
	2	Observing for pattern/comparison	
	3	Observing for change	recognise observable changes in events, motion and time.
	4	Using an appropriate method for observation	select equipment, instruments or sensory information for the purpose of a particular observation.
FAMILY—INTERPRETATION	5	Sorting items into order	sort items into order.
	6	Grouping items according to specified criteria	group items according to specified criteria.
	7	Tabulating information	arrange information in an orderly manner.
	8	Using tables of information	extract and use information given in a tabular form.
	9	Using classification systems	use classification systems.
	10	Drawing representational and scale diagrams, plans or maps	draw representational and scale diagrams, plans or maps.
	11	Interpreting and using representational and scale diagrams, plans or maps	interpret and use representational and scale diagrams, plans or maps.
FAMILY – PROBLEM SOLVING	12	Identify a problem	recognise and describe the nature of simple environmental, social and practical problems.
	13	Asking questions (i) from observation	gain information using several senses.
		(ii) from investigating	gain information by practical exploration
	14	Proposing reasons	collect, relate and sort evidence for possible causes.
	15	Selecting likely explanations	select probable causes and their effects from a range of possibilities and select most likely explanations.
			recognise limitations.
	16	Testing likely explanations	check explanations by a variety of procedures.
	17	Implementing solutions	describe/carry out appropriate procedures in order to solve problems.
	18	Monitoring the outcomes of solutions	assess the outcome of their problem solving.

Descriptive Assessments

Descriptive assessments resemble the traditional style of report familiar to many students, parents and teachers. Teachers are likely to be confident in using this recording method because it is familiar to them. Its potential for providing considerable detail which is easily understood should also promote effective discussion and negotiation about assessment.

Like other methods it has its problems: completing descriptive assessments can be extremely time-consuming and writing precise, detailed and diagnostic reports linked to the curriculum objectives of a particular department is a skill which so far only a few teachers have developed. A large-scale in-service programme would therefore be needed by most teachers if such a method were widely used, and they would also need to find the necessary writing time. A more detailed analysis and examples of descriptive assessments can be found in Chapter 7.

Self-assessments

The development of student self-assessment is more likely to lead to effective discussion between teacher and student and the development of negotiation. Self-evaluation is an important skill and an essential precondition to dialogue within the profiling process. It has, of course, large-scale implications for any institution adopting it.

To regard the student as a real partner in the educational process means giving him or her decision-making responsibilities. This has an effect on the traditional teacher-student relationship. To avoid severe problems change should not occur without adequate preparation and training both for students and teachers.

The skills of self-evaluation can occur at different levels at any age. The principle of partnership between teacher and pupil can exist in the primary classroom. However, in primary and secondary schools the teacher and the pupils are not equal partners: the educational process rightly remains the responsibility of the teacher. As the student progresses, he or she can benefit from taking an increasing responsibility in the assessment process and for his or her own learning. In the secondary school, teachers and students should discuss progress and achievements fully, but it is unlikely that full negotiation on learning objectives can or should occur. There may, however, be further education programmes and schemes within the Manpower Services Commission through which full negotiation can be developed appropriately. The Internal Report from Bosworth College shown opposite reveals a quite open and unstructured response. On the reverse side of the document are guidelines to help parents interpret this. The needlework profile shown on page 57, developed in a Dorset school during piloting phases, is a more structured approach within a subject frame of reference.

CROSS-CURRICULAR SKILLS

What are the criteria for assessment?

In recent years emphasis has been placed on the development of cross-curricular skills. These are skills needed and used frequently in a variety of learning situations. So that students can progress, cross-curricular skills must be developed within a structured programme.

Several different classifications of such skills have been developed over recent years. The HMI document *Curriculum 11–16: Towards a Statement of Entitlement* lists them as

Communication
Numerical
Observational and visual
Imaginative
Organisational and study
Physical and practical
Social
Problem-solving
Creative

osworth College   **Internal Report**

Name	Date of birth	Div & T.G.	Subject & course

Student's Self Assessment   Date

Bosworth College   Parents' Copy   Staff Assessment

Name	Date of birth	Div & T.G.	Subject & course

Staff Name   Date

Examination prospects on present performance

	O	CSE	A	CEE
strong	strong	strong	strong	strong
average	average	average	average	average
weak	weak	weak	weak	weak
ungraded	ungraded	ungraded	likely fail	

NEEDLEWORK PROFILE

**Read the sections carefully then tick the boxes which you think apply to you.
There is a line for your own comment if you wish to make one.**

1. HANDSEWING
Do I know how to make the following:
Straight neat tacking
Hem a skirt
Gather stitching
Prepare dart
Work two or more embroidery stitches etc?

2. MACHINE WORK
Can I thread a sewing machine correctly?
Can I adjust a machine if it isn't sewing correctly?
Can I machine a straight line?
Can I use a zig-zag stitch?

3. TEXTILES
Do I know how the following are made:-
Cotton, Linen, Wool, Silk, Man-made fabrics etc?
Do I know about the different finishes available?
The cost of fabrics?
Different weaves, textures and laundry methods
for these fabrics?

4. HISTORY OF CLOTHES
Do I visit costume museums?
Do I collect costume dolls from foreign countries?
Am I interested in the clothes my grandparents
and their parents wore etc?

5. TODAY'S FASHIONS
Do I copy and make any of the following:-
Latest styles in skirts, blouses, dresses,
jackets etc?
Do I alter any other clothes to make them more
interesting and fashionable?
Do I alter jeans and skirt lengths to make them
more suitable to wear?

6. MAKING TOYS
Do I make any soft toys for myself or family?
Have I used felt, can I manage to use fur fabric
to make toys?
Do I know about different types of stuffing?
Do I know about safety features involved?

**7. HOUSEHOLD
FURNISHINGS**
Have I made any of the following:-
Cushions, curtains, bean bags etc?
Have I altered any of my bedroom furnishings?

8. OTHER NEEDLEWORK
Do I enjoy knitting
crocheting
rugmaking?
Perhaps I prefer to make lampshades

or macramé
or even lacemaking
patchwork
quilting
tapestry

or appliqué pictures?

Name .... Form .... Date ....

Departments should discuss

which skills are used within the specific curriculum, and

which skills are not effectively promoted but need to be if effective learning is to take place.

Each department will then need to consider whether effective measures are taken to promote the skills within the curriculum objectives and whether they are regularly assessed.

What is the most appropriate method of assessment for each of the chosen criteria?

There must be flexibility in determining the most appropriate method of assessment for each of the criteria. This is because cross-curricular skills are diverse and developed in very different contexts. For example, the skill of observation may be promoted very differently in the science laboratory and in the art room and so needs to be assessed accordingly.

The method selected must reveal the information required, namely, whether the designated skill is being developed across a variety of learning experiences. It would be very important to discover, for example, that a skill was being successfully developed by a student in certain situations but unsuccessfully in others. If so, you should ask

(1) Why is the skill developed in this situation but not in that?

(2) Is this the result of student performance or the learning experience? and

(3) What action can be taken to remedy the position and to provide the student with assistance in weaker areas?

It is very useful for teachers and departments to share their experiences of how to assess cross-curricular skills. If some departments are reluctant to use a particular method because staff are not competent or confident to use it, discussions with colleagues who do use it may provide the very help required. For example, it may be that particular observation skills are used successfully in the drama department and these skills could be shared with members of the science department who also wish to observe learning situations.

How is the information to be recorded?

The first question to be considered is whether a departmental profile should be extended to include the necessary cross-curricular components or whether a cross-curricular profile should be used across the departments. If a departmental profile is used, the departmental recording method must be followed. If a cross-curricular profile is used, a common recording method will be used throughout the institution.

The most common recording methods used are the progress grid and the checklist. Both methods act as templates across a variety of learning situations. However, there is no reason why any other method of recording student progress and achievements should not be used for the assessment of cross-curricular skills.

Progress Grids

The most common system of profiling used in this country is the Progress Profile Report of the CGLI shown in Chapter 1. It is concerned with the promotion and assessment of cross-curricular skills. The space against each criterion allows the teacher to show each context within which the student performance took place.

Another progress grid for recording information about cross-curricular skills is shown opposite and used in the profile of the Newton High School, Powys, based on the model developed for the Scottish Pupils in Profile Project.

Checklists

The RSA has developed a series of checklists for practical skills designed to act as templates across a variety of courses and learning experiences. This approach provides a precise focus for discussion between departments, and between teachers and students but produces a major problem concerning the level of achievement in relation to the context in which the skill was displayed. If someone reading such a profile has no knowledge of how the skill was displayed, he or she will not know with what level of competency it was carried out. Many people believe that there should therefore be a minimum standard of competency shown before credit is given for that skill. Alternatively the context may be provided by a course

LISTENING

Acts independently and intelligently on complex and verbal instructions ☐

Can interpret and act on most complex instructions ☐

Can interpret and act on straightforward instructions ☐

Can carry out simple instructions with supervision ☐

READING

Understands all appropriate written material ☐

Understands the content and implications of most writing if simply expressed ☐

Understands uncomplicated ideas expressed in simple language ☐

Can read most everyday information such as notices or simple instructions ☐

VISUAL UNDERSTANDING

Can communicate complex visual concepts readily and appropriately ☐

Can give a clear explanation by sketches and diagrams ☐

Can interpret a variety of visual displays such as graphs or train timetables ☐

Can interpret single visual displays such as road signs or outline maps ☐

PHYSICAL EDUCATION

MANUAL DEXTERITY

Can achieve complex practical tasks ☐

Has an understanding of instructions both written and oral, and carry out the required task ☐

Is able to perform useful practical tasks under instruction ☐

Can achieve simple practical tasks ☐

SPEAKING

Can debate a point of view ☐

Can make a clear and accurate report ☐

Can describe events orally ☐

Can communicate adequately at conversation level ☐

WRITING

Can argue a point of view ☐

Can write a clear and accurate report ☐

Can write a simple account or letter ☐

Can write simple messages and instructions ☐

USE OF NUMBER

Quick and accurate in complicated or unfamiliar calculations ☐

Can do familiar or straightforward calculations, more slowly if complex ☐

Can handle routine calculations with practice ☐

Can do simple whole number calculations such as giving change ☐

....

....

description which could identify clearly how the skills would be displayed.

Examples of checklists are the RSA Practical Communication Skills Profile, shown overleaf and on page 62, and the language, maths, practical and personal and social skills extract from the Evesham profile on pages 63–4 which has been very influential in school developments.

Practical Communication Skills Profile

The Student has demonstrated the ability to:

A *Dealing with People*

1. Establish working relationships with individuals
2. Establish working relationships as a member of a group
3. Relay given information orally to an individual
4. Relay given information orally to a group
5. Ask questions in order to obtain information for a specific purpose
6. Make and carry out arrangements in accordance with a stated goal
7. Give instructions in order that a particular task can be completed
8. Take instructions in order that a particular task can be completed
9. Describe an object, person or event accurately
10. Explain a process or sequence of events so that it can be followed
11. Open, conduct and close a brief transaction face to face
12. Open, conduct and close a brief transaction by telephone
13. Listen to points of view presented in discussion re-state them accurately
14. State own point of view clearly in discussion
15. Distinguish fact from opinion during discussion
16. Judge the validity of arguments presented orally
17. Express disagreement without provoking hostility in discussion
18. Participate effectively in negotiation

B *Dealing with Information*

1. Read straightforward printed texts and extract the information required
2. Read straightforward clear handwritten texts and extract the information required
3. Read a letter, detailed notice, leaflet, pamphlet or short article in printed form

4. Read a letter or detailed notice in clear handwritten form

5. Read texts containing complex sentences and sophisticated vocabulary

6. Scan written material to locate required information

7. Skim written material and convey the gist

8. Use alphabetical order and index systems to locate information in dictionaries and reference books

9. Locate information in a library or filing system for a stated purpose

10. Transfer information accurately

11. Check written material for errors and discrepancies

12. Interpret and make use of pictorial and graphic information such as pictures, diagrams, graphs, tables, maps, dials, gauges*

13. Present information in pictorial or graphic form so that is can be used by others

14. Make notes from written and spoken material

15. Relay accurately a given piece of spoken information in writing

16. Adapt information into an appropriate format for a stated purpose

17. Use appropriate content and expression in writing

18. Produce a simple report of a given situation or event to convey the essential facts to others

19. Produce formal and informal letters

20. Complete a variety of forms accurately and legibly

21. Carry out everyday financial transactions (e.g. receive and transfer money through cheques and giros)

22. File information systematically so that a specific item can be located

23. Retrieve information from computer based sources (e.g. viewdata, teletext, word processors)

*Students should show evidence in at least four of the suggested media for this sentence to be credited.

Note Items inside the brackets appear for teachers, but not on the profile certificates

The Evesham Profile

LANGUAGE SKILLS	Staff	Date	Stamp	MATHS SKILLS	Staff	Date	Stamp
1. Has legible handwriting				1. Has a good understanding of the rules of number			
2. Can write simple sentences				2. Has a good accuracy in handling numbers			
3. Can read and understand a popular newspaper				3. Can apply the four rules to money with accuracy			
4. Can use simple punctuation correctly				4. Capable of performing every-day calculations in money accurate			
5. Avoids elementary spelling mistakes				5. Understands money transactions such as wages and income tax			
6. Can write a personal letter				6. Able to handle decimals met in everyday life			
7. Can give and take a telephone message				7. Able to handle fractions met in everyday life			
8. Can accurately complete a passport application				8. Understands simple percentages			
9. Regularly borrows from school or public library				9. Understands simple profit and loss			
10. Can write a business letter				10. Understands metric system of measure			
11. Can make an accurate written report				11. Understands English measures of length, weight and capacity			
12. Can make a clear spoken report				12. Can measure accurately			
13. Can summarise accurately a notice or report				13. Is able to use a calculator			
14. Can understand simple instructions in a foreign language				14. Has an understanding of V.A.T.			
15. Can give simple instructions in a foreign language				15. Can read & understand time-tables, wage tables & ready reckoner			

PRACTICAL SKILLS	Staff	Date	Stamp	PERSONAL SKILLS	Staff	Date	Stamp
1. Is aware of safety precautions in the home				1. Is normally and cleanly dressed for school			
2. Is aware of safety precautions in the workshop				2. Is normally punctual			
3. Is aware of safety precautions in the laboratory				3. Has a good attendance record			
4. Can use correctly a domestic washing machine				4. Takes a pride in his/her work			
5. Can iron correctly a shirt or dress				5. Can work well without close supervision			
6. Can use correctly a domestic sewing machine				6. Can work well as a member of a group			
7. Is competent in basic cookery				7. Can organise his/her work efficiently			
8. Can use appropriate hand tools correctly				8. Has played for school team			
9. Can make 3 simple joints in wood or metal				9. Can swim 25 m			
10. Can understand a working drawing or pattern				10. Is a regular member of a school club or society			
11. Can express ideas in sketch or diagram form				11. Has attended a school residential course or expedition			
12. Can choose and follow a route or a map				12. Can receive and escort school visitors			
13. Can type accurately at 20 w.p.m.				13. Has taken part in school or year assemblies			
14. Understands scientific terms in common use				14. Has had a position of responsibility at school			
15. Understands technical terms in common use				15. Shows a capacity for organisation and leadership			

PERSONAL AND SOCIAL SKILLS

What are the criteria for assessment?

Personal and social skills are closely related to cross-curricular skills but, unlike them, are not solely dependent on the formal curriculum objectives and learning programmes of an institution. These skills can also be derived from the hidden curriculum and the ethos of the institution. This distinction may seem to be artificial but it is important. The design of the profile must take account of the full spectrum of learning experiences and should include the full range of skills used by the student, but the recording system need not have separate components for cross-curricular and personal and social skills provided that due consideration is given to both types.

This has been achieved in the proposals for the CPVE which are based on the concept that the core of the curriculum objectives should reflect content and provide the opportunity for the students to develop the skills and attitudes seen as essential throughout all the learning experiences. In other words, the core is not a body of knowledge which is a separate component, but a range of skills, knowledge, attitudes and concepts which must be promoted within any particular learning programme. This core reflects the importance of both cross-curricular and personal and social skills.

CPVE CORE

Personal and social developments

Communication

Numeracy

Science and technology

Industrial, social and economic studies

Information technology

Skills for learning, decision making and adaptability

Practical skills

Social skills

Creative development

There are several profiles where personal and social skills criteria comprise a separate section. One such example is the Clwyd profile shown on page 74, where the social relationships' criteria are a compromise between those skills or qualities which employers would find useful and those which teachers would be confident about assessing. On the other hand, the criteria from the School Technology Forum 'Pupil Profiles and Transferable Skills' shown below contain those skills or qualities seen to be necessary for a successful working life.

CLWYD SCHOOL TECHNOLOGY FORUM		
Adaptability	MOTIVATION	– Persistence
		Perseverance
Perseverance		Determination
Initiative	SOCIAL QUALITIES	– Reliability – dependable
		Cooperation – team work
Self-confidence		Working with others
Leadership	RATIONAL THINKING	– Express a logical argument
	and REASONING	Make sensible decisions
Social		Consider causes of action
Relationships		Justify actions – exercise
		judgement
Attendance		
	ADAPTABILITY AND	– Face change in work,
Punctuality	FLEXIBILITY	organisation and environment
		Modify ideas, views and actions
	INITIATIVE/	– Make decisions and take action
	INDEPENDENCE/	with minimal supervision
	RESOURCEFULNESS	Work independently
		Improvise with available
		resources
	ATTITUDES	– Cleanliness
		Tidiness
		Honesty
		Integrity
		Personal commitment
		Safety and consideration for
		others
	DISCIPLINE/	– Accept leadership and
	SELF-DISCIPLINE/	supervision
	SELF-ORGANISATION	Organise personal actions
		Punctuality, neatness,
		organisation and self-control

What is the most appropriate method of assessment for each of the chosen criteria?

In Chapter 5 we recommended that you should assess personal 'skills' rather than personal 'qualities' as advocated in the policy statement of the DES. This distinction is critical because assessment of personal qualities is extremely difficult, even if desirable, and is neither predictive nor capable of generalisation.

There should be a clear declaration of the personal and social skills which the institution is attempting to promote in co-operation with the students. The teacher should structure the learning experiences in such a way that these skills can be developed and then gather specific evidence of how the student performed in that context in response to those skills so that assessment can be made. The assessment is therefore related to a specific task and is based on precise evidence. Throughout the development work two questions reappear

'What do I wish the student to learn or develop?'

'What evidence have I that this learning has taken place?'

Assessments of personal and social skills are likely to be based on methods that are largely observational, structured or informal. It is important that they should *not* be made by only one member of staff but should be discussed with and by a variety of staff who know the student well and engage in different relationships in different contexts. Their various reponses should not be reduced to a single interpretation of performance but differences should be highlighted instead. The assessment must be discussed in detail with the student so that he or she can understand how others may have different perceptions and what the reasons may be. The assessment must bring about self-reflection leading to increased self-awareness by the student.

Many teachers have been concerned about the possibility of abusing the integrity of students by including personal and social skills in a profile but the following three guiding principles should avoid any such problems.

(1) The assessments should refer to specific goals and objectives which can be clearly identified by all concerned.

(2) The assessments should be clearly supported by evidence which is understood by the student.

(3) The student should be fully involved in the discussion and where possible the negotiation of the assessments. There is much to be gained from the use of student self-assessment in evaluating performance in response to stated goals.

These principles should help the student to understand the assessments fully and to develop and understand his or her performance in response to a full range of learning experiences promoted by the institution. Nevertheless it is vital to be sensitive when assessing, recording and having discussions with students in order to protect their integrity and dignity.

How is the information to be recorded?

Any method of recording could be used to record information on personal and social skills but some, such as grading or progress grids, may lack sensitivity and therefore be inappropriate. The appropriate alternatives are

Student self-assessment

Descriptive assessments

Statements of achievements or experiences

Comment banks

Student Self-assessment

Self-assessment encourages self-reflection and gives the student an increased feeling of involvement in the assessment and learning process. Self-assessment may also let the teacher see what the student's real feelings are towards the learning objectives and the learning programme. In the classroom, teachers can very often gain incorrect impressions about student attitudes to work.

The Barnsley summary of attitudes, relationships and basic skills shown overleaf shows how a student can become fully involved in the assessment process and how self-assessment placed next to teacher assessment can lead to effective dialogue. (This profile has been superseded by alternative versions.)

	Assessment of Student by Staff			Student's Self Assessment		
	Rarely	Sometimes	Usually	Rarely	Sometimes	Usually

SUMMARY OF ATTITUDES AND RELATIONSHIPS DEMONSTRATED DURING COURSE

1. Appreciates a need for a flexible outlook and adopts it
2. Justifiably self confident
3. Sensitive to needs of others
4. Shows initiative when appropriate
5. Co-operates with peers
6. Co-operates with staff
7. Shows leadership potential
8. Accepts conventions of appropriate dress and behaviour
9. Sustains concentration and effort
10. Willing to participate in discussions
11. Willingly tackles worksheet : Vocational Studies
    Core Studies
12. Willingly undertakes extra work related to: Vocational Studies
    Core Studies
13. Presents work attractively in a variety of ways
14. Maintains a balance between academic work and other interests

OTHERS

SUMMARY OF BASIC SKILLS DEMONSTRATED DURING COURSE

15. Clear powers of Oral Expression
16. Clear powers of Written Expression
17. Used information retrieval systems
18. Accurate with Mathematical Calculations
19. Can read and understand data presented in various forms
20. Can receive and follow instructions given orally

OTHERS

Attendance: _____ Punctuality: Good/Poor Health: Normal/Not Normal

TUTOR'S COMMENT

Signature: _____ Course Tutor

Institution: _____
Telephone: _____

Work Experience Report Attached.

STUDENT'S COMMENT

Signature: _____
Moderator: _____

Descriptive Assessments

The DES policy statement believes that assessments of personal and social skills should be optional. Any such assessments should observe the following guidelines.

(1) Assessments should attempt to give a fair and reasonable view displayed over a period of time and should only concern activities in school about which teachers have direct knowledge.

(2) Assessments should only refer to positive qualities.

(3) Assessments should be supported by concrete examples.

(4) Assessments should be recorded in sentences and not by means of grades or ticks in boxes.

The key question which any teacher should ask is *'What evidence do I have to support that judgement?'*

Many teachers claim to have experience of descriptive assessments from completing the tutor's section of parental reports but those statements are often subjective and are not based upon a full spectrum of experiences.

The assessment from Lea Manor High School on pages 71 and 72 seems to satisfy the guidelines but the Tutor's Assessment could perhaps be improved by more concrete examples to substantiate some of the points made.

Statements of Achievements or Experiences

The DES policy statement states that this method should always be used.

'The nature and coverage of this component in the summary document of record is more debateable. It seems clear that the inclusion of personal accounts by pupils themselves of their activities or experiences . . . should be optional. The factual, or largely factual, list of achievements and experiences . . . on the other hand should always be included. It should be accompanied wherever possible by a brief commentary drawing attention to any special factors, such as any limitations on the range of opportunities available to a pupil, and giving credit for effort and hard work as well as actual attainments. The objective should be to throw light on the personal qualities which underlie the achievements listed.'

Tutor's Assessment

_____   **Registration Group 5B**

Interests and Leisure Pursuits

_____ has many varied and interesting leisure activities including being an enthusiastic and capable sportsman and having a genuine interest in the arts. He is able to relax in the company of most people and can talk confidently about a wide number of different topics. He has participated fully in all the varied aspects of school life and has been a regular member of the School Football and Basketball teams as well as being the outstanding distance runner in his age group. He has also been willing to freely give of his time to help out at a variety of school functions.

Experiences of Work

_____ did not have the opportunity to complete a period of work experience but his mature approach to life leads us to think that he will have little difficulty in making the transition from school to full-time employment. _____ has greatly impressed staff with his ability to apply himself to the numerous demands of his examination courses. He has worked hard over the last 2 years and has already gained a GCE grade A in English Language.

Character and Personal Qualities

_____ 's attendance and punctuality records have been excellent throughout his stay at Lea Manor. He is a mature person, with a clear and confident, friendly manner, who has enjoyed very good relationships with staff and pupils alike. He has always been completely reliable and his standard of appearance has been a credit to the school. _____ has been form captain and prefect and has carried out his duties with great success. We therefore feel confident that _____ will use his talents to the full and prove to be an invaluable asset to any future employer. _____ 's contribution to the life and atmosphere of Lea Manor has been tremendous and will be greatly missed; we wish him every success in his future career.

Pupil's Assessment

Interests and Leisure Activities

Liking to keep myself quite active I do a lot of sport including basketball, football, swimming, table tennis, badminton, squash, and athletics. These are just casual except football which is for the school as well as basketball and athletics. I also play football for the Sacred Heart Football Club. At home, I enjoy watching television, home computing, reading, drawing and listening to music. I belong to quite a large family and we go to church and various clubs together. I go out quite often with friends to town but not as often as I used to in an attempt to concentrate on homework.

Experiences of Work

I enjoy reading and writing, especially in English. Also I like debates where I can express my opinions. I listen to people well and carry out instructions competently and reliably. My interests are electronics and art at home and I change plugs, look at tape recorders and change fuses. Also I sketch and draw at home especially liking surrealistic and imaginative work. In the past I enjoyed playing the recorder and can still read music. I do the usual jobs at home such as washing up, tidying up and hoovering. My experiences of writing at home are doing the pools, writing programs on my computer and puzzle books. I plan things quite carefully always trying to keep a note of my homework. I am never late for school and have very few days off.

Character and Personal Qualities

I think I am a fairly outgoing sort of person who gets on well with people of all ages. With people I do not know, I try to get to talk to them but am a little shy. Also if speaking in front of an audience or crowd I am embarrassed at first but as time goes on I begin to enjoy it. I am cooperative in most situations trying to see all points of view. Sometimes, I tend to fix an idea in my head and do not like it changed. I enjoy being with other people and especially like humour as my own sense of humour is good. Also, I like to be alone sometimes and listen to music to get away from the bustle of my house especially with a three year old brother. I have good leadership qualities having been captain of a five-a-side team, house teams (organising sports), and I am currently Deputy Head Boy. I am reliable and carry out my duties well. My manner is talkative most times but quiet sometimes and I am confident. I like to look smart every day and keep myself clean and tidy.

Such a method has advantages by being *simple to operate* and by *avoiding very difficult subjective judgements in sensitive areas*. But the relationship between appropriate activities or experiences and specific personal qualities or skills can cause a problem and it can be difficult for anyone using the summary record to identify such qualities or skills from the activities listed. Any activity involves the use of a variety of overlapping skills and/or qualities some of which may have been successfully displayed whilst others may have been neglected. For example, is it clear what skills or qualities would be required to be Treasurer of the School Dramatic Society? Is it possible to discover from a factual statement of this kind whether the student was a successful Treasurer, or whether the student had developed certain specific qualities or skills but had not developed others?

Comment Banks

Difficulties caused by subjectivity and the need for sensitivity have led some teachers to develop comment banks for recording personal and social skills. Their use need not be restricted to these skills.

In a comment bank, the teacher selects the most appropriate sentences for each student from a series of statements. The statements are standard for all the students and the system therefore lends itself to being computerised. This can save time for teachers and secretarial staff when completing the profiles although more time is needed to prepare the program to operate the scheme.

The comment bank method does not solve the problem of having to select an appropriate assessment which is valid and reliable. The teacher still needs to consider which statements give appropriate credit for the full range of evidence which the student has displayed over all the learning experiences. The method is not helpful if there are no appropriate sentences for an individual student. The example of the Clwyd comment bank on social relationships all too clearly illustrates the problems.

PUPIL PROFILE
RESPONSE TO OTHERS

1. A cheerful and tolerant nature makes X a delight to be with

2. X is a popular and central figure with a wide circle of friends.

3. X's confident and easy assurance enables him/her to relate to other people well.

4. X is always well-mannered and courteous.

5. X is able to form and maintain very good relationships with his/her fellow pupils and adults.

6. One of the attractive features of X's personality is a lively sense of humour.

7. X often takes the initiative as a sensible spokesperson for a group and is a good organiser.

8. He/she often shows particular concern for others.

9. The openness and honesty of X's relationships enable him/her to solve a conflict situation sensibly and successfully.

10. X has shown him/herself to be a thoroughly responsible and trustworthy person.

11. X is generally accepted by his/her fellow pupils.

12. X knows when to seek support from adults in resolving conflict situations.

13. X is able to form and maintain generally good relationships with adults.

14. If called upon, X has shown that he/she can be a sensible spokesperson.

15. Most of the time X is well mannered and courteous.

16. X has proved him/herself to be generally trustworthy and/or responsible.

17. Within a small group X is able to form generally good relationships.

18. Although X can mix well with his/her fellow pupils, he/she prefers his/her own company.

19. X is normally well-mannered, but he/she has on occasions appeared discourteous.

20. While getting on well with his/her own group of friends, X finds difficulty in forming relationships with other people.

21. X is a popular figure but he/she occasionally shows some lack of self-control.

22. X is capable of leadership but does not always use his/her position responsibly.

23. X occasionally finds difficulty in resolving conflicts amicably.

24. X can voice his/her opinion well, but does not always do so responsibly.

25. X has good relationships with adults but finds it very difficult to get on with his/her fellow pupils.

26. Relationships with others can be spoiled by X's lack of self restraint.

27. X gets on well with his/her fellow pupils, but is often in conflict with adults.

ACHIEVEMENTS AND EXPERIENCES

What are the criteria for assessment?

Some teachers claim that only those achievements and experiences which have been provided directly by the school or college in the formal curriculum and through extra-curricular activities can be validated and included in a record of achievement.

Others claim that for some students the most meaningful learning experiences occur outside the control or even the knowledge of their teachers and, if the record of achievement is to reveal the full range of achievements and experiences, then they should be included, provided that their authenticity is validated in some way. A powerful case can also be made for the inclusion of achievements and experiences from outside school or college on the grounds that they will help to provide a full picture of the abilities, experiences, interests and needs of each student. There are occasions when experiences gained from outside can add an important dimension to understanding a student's performance in relation to the structured objectives of the curriculum.

A range of achievements and experiences may therefore legitimately be included to reflect a student's interests, activities, pursuits, pastimes and endeavours. Some of these, such as sports, music or outdoor pursuits, may be the subject of awards from outside agencies.

What is the most appropriate method of assessment for each of the chosen criteria?

Many profile achievements and experiences cannot be assessed traditionally and will simply be recorded as statements of fact. There may not even be any self-assessment of such achievements and experiences.

Other experiences may be judged and assessed within strict guidelines established by an external accrediting agency as, for example, with the British Amateur Gymnastics Awards or the Duke of Edinburgh Award schemes.

There may, however, be certain school-directed or college-directed activities, such as Work Experience and Residential Experience, where benefit could come from assessment. The student may want feedback here and such assessment is more likely to be based on informal methods including observation.

The example of Work Experience highlights several problems: the observation techniques are often undeveloped, especially for certain learning situations, and the assessment may be carried out by someone from outside the school. These problems provoke the questions

'Who is to be involved in the assessment process?' and

'What guidance should be given to the student, teachers, employer or parent to help them in the learning process?'

How is the information to be recorded?

There are a number of possible methods of recording achievements and experiences.

A descriptive account or list of statements

Student personal recording

Assessment schedules for Work Experience

External or internal certificates

Descriptive Account
This could be a descriptive statement of achievements and experiences completed from the information available to the school or college staff, or it could result from a process of negotiation between the student and tutors. An example of a descriptive account has already been seen in the assessment from Lea Manor High School, shown on pages 71–2.

Student Personal Recording
There are many teachers who have experience of personal recording over a period of nearly 20 years and would claim that there are important aspects of human development which cannot be assessed by another person. Only the student can declare which specific

achievements and experiences are meaningful to him or her and sometimes a particular experience may not have been recognised as meaningful even though it may have had a most marked effect on the student. These teachers would claim through experience gained from schemes such as the Record of Personal Achievement, the Record of Personal Experience and Pupils' Personal Records that it is only the student who can make a realistic, effective and valid contribution to this section of the Record of Achievement.

These three schemes allow individual recording of personal achievements or experiences on pre-titled cards (see opposite). The process is entirely student-directed in terms of the content, style, presentation and ultimate destination of the record. *It is the absolute property of the student.* Tutors involved in such schemes require particular skills which need to be developed through In Service Education and Training (INSET) support programmes.

Personal recording has influenced many teachers and can exist as part of local developments without full involvement in any national scheme. We believe that personal recording can provide an important and often vital dimension to the development of a record of achievement. It cannot of itself, however, constitute that record because it may not reflect the full range of learning experiences and has no assessment or perception from the teacher.

Assessment Schedules for Work Experience

Some school-directed experiences may be appropriately assessed. Many students take part in Work Experience without any formal evaluation of their experience in the workplace. Many schools have designed schedules to assist students in such an evaluation and to help them to understand how their performance was viewed by an employer or supervisor.

Such an assessment schedule would generally not be used directly in the record of achievement but more in the formative learning process. It might, however, reveal information which could be translated into a statement for the record of achievement.

The example given on page 79 was piloted in a Dorset school. The same schedule is completed independently by the student and the

AWAY FROM HOME & EXPEDITIONS

DATE FROM	TO
PLACE	
MEANS OF TRANSPORT	
TYPE OF ACCOMODATION	
ACTIVITY	

NAME

SIGNED	POSITION	DATE

| Name of Employer | | Name of Student | |
| Nature of Work | | Supervisor | |

SKILL OR QUALITY	Tick if the Quality was displayed	Comment or give examples if it is appropriate
JOB SPECIFIC SKILLS Aptitude for the work Ability to work methodically Enthusiasm Inquiring mind Pride in job Ability to follow instructions Ability to work in a team Ability to produce work of quality		
PERSONAL AND SOCIAL SKILLS Appearance Time-keeping Reliability Adaptability Initiative Common sense Perseverance Concentration Self-confidence Politeness Healthy attitude to authority Ability to accept criticism Ability to mix with colleagues		

Further Comments

Dates of Work Experience

employer or supervisor on completion of Work Experience. The tutor then uses the evidence to talk with the student about his or her performance. A similar approach could be used for residential experiences.

External or Internal Certificates

It is surprising how diverse many students' interests and activities can be. Success in many of these activities is rewarded by the presentation of certificates for achievements in, for example, sporting activities, the arts, charitable endeavours, hobbies and leisure pursuits, and students generally take great pride in owning them.

A school or college may wish to consider whether these certificates should be included in the summative record of achievement by designing it to hold such documents in addition to examination certificates.

PULLING IT ALL TOGETHER

It is unimportant whether a school or college has used its own profile components or those suggested earlier, namely

 Subject or course assessment
 Cross-curricular skills
 Personal and social skills
 Achievements and experiences

The structure outlined earlier has been designed to help you to classify what might be included both in a formative recording system and in a summative record of achievement. You will also need to decide

 Whether the components used in the formative profile and the summative record of achievement are to be the same

 Whether the main criteria of each component will be identical

 How the information revealed in the formative profile can be condensed into a short record of achievement without losing the individual nature of the record but still maintaining the full breadth of achievements and experiences.

The constituent parts of the profile must be considered as a whole package. This is particularly significant for the formative profile. There are a number of key characteristics which need to be delivered in order to ensure that it is coherent and consistent.The profile must

(1) Reveal the full breadth of the learning experience

(2) Possess balance, without repetition or gaps

(3) Be relevant to the learning needs of the student

(4) Aid the learning development of the student by providing for continuity and progression

(5) Assist the teacher by providing information which is useful for the evaluation of teaching

(6) Contain no information which will not be used by the student and the teacher

(7) Fulfil the original aims of the school or course

Chapter 7

ASSESSMENT

CREATING AN ASSESSMENT MODEL

What do we mean when we say 'Assessment is central to the whole teaching-learning process'? What we are really saying is that most of the characteristics of a good teacher or student depend on quality assessment. Such characteristics include the ability to

Ask pertinent questions
Listen attentively to what is being said
Observe closely what is happening
Identify learning blockages, and
Take speedy and appropriate action to remedy them

Hence competence and experience in this area constitute a major weapon in any successful teacher's armoury.

More than any other of the government's current 'examination' initiatives – which it sees incidentally as the key to curriculum control – profiles, if they are to succeed, require assessment to be totally integrated within the processes of preparation, implementation and delivery of the curriculum. It is hardly surprising, therefore, that this book has been littered with references to assessment. It is not surprising either that the major problem in achieving this integration is one of attitude.

Changing attitudes cannot of course remain solely an in-service responsibility. Pre-service provision needs to be significantly reappraised in this area and three matters need particular consideration.

(1) Programmes of assessment should be developed for students under training which evaluate their performance and show them how their own assessment can be used in positive terms to help both them and those who teach them. Every student leaving a

training establishment with the view that his or her assessment was something just to be undergone and then forgotten, results in another teacher with a potentially negative attitude to assessment.

(2) Students under training need to be able to know what kind of assessment can be used for particular purposes and what uses can legitimately be made of the results of any particular assessment.

(3) Instruction in course-planning should stress the importance of building in assessment for evaluation purposes at the planning stage.

None of these changes need significantly increase the overall time demands on pre-service courses. They would, however, significantly improve the platform of confidence and competence on which institutions could subsequently build their in-service training. Incidentally it is not necessary in pre-service training to place great emphasis on assessment construction: the necessary skills here are best developed on the ground. It is the one area of assessment, moreover, where there is no shortage of relevant instructional material.

Given that changes of the kind suggested will not be implemented overnight, any institution embarking on the development of profiles will first have to decide how to alter attitudes to assessment. Two recent and interrelated developments will help here.

Much greater stress is being given to performance criteria as the basis for student assessment and, to a lesser extent, course and curriculum assessment.

There is the desire to extend the range of information available about young people when they leave full-time education.

Of these the first is the most important since it represents a fundamental shift in the basis of comparison within assessment from norm to criterion referencing (see page 12). This means that the emphasis has been moved from comparisons between individuals, which usually operate to someone's disadvantage ('I am an A, he or she is a B'), to comparisons between individuals and agreed criteria. These will have been specified in advance, ideally as a result of wide-ranging national or local debate which has achieved consensus.

This shift is much less easy to make in education than it is in, say, training because there is a lack of reference points both inside and outside the education system against which to establish performance criteria. Thus the criteria used are essentially arbitrary and it is difficult to establish what constitutes both appropriate criteria and appropriate performances in relation to criteria. There is moreover no such thing as pure criterion referencing in education where the desire, and often the need, to make comparisons between individuals is deep-rooted. Despite these problems, this shift has the following significant implications for those concerned to change attitudes.

(1) It emphasises the positive side of assessment.

(2) It encourages the development of a bottom-up model (see page 107) for assessment and hence addresses the key issue of progression.

(3) It underlines the unhelpfulness of marks or grades.

The desire to extend the range of information also has a number of important consequences for changing attitudes.

(4) It encourages more descriptive assessment in which the descriptions are simply validated by whoever is in the best position to do this.

(5) It involves a greater range of people in the assessment process including those being assessed.

(6) It involves a greater emphasis on informal rather than on formal assessment over a period rather than at one particular time.

Although they are not an exhaustive list, these six points create a model for assessment which is very different from those currently used in schools, and one which can only be operated with the wholehearted co-operation of teachers. Withers and Cornish in a significant paper published in May 1984 (see page 141) call such a model 'non-competitive' and argue that it will permit assessment to

Facilitate curricula that are student-centred rather than systems-based and hence responsive to the needs and abilities of both teacher and student

Promote individual development

Be co-operative in nature

Provide assistance to students

Be useful in placing individuals

This represents the kind of assessment model that ought to be aimed at by those wanting to introduce and operate profiles. But how can such a model be achieved *in practice*? What methods of assessment should be chosen from those available?

FITNESS FOR PURPOSE

Extensive criteria for assessment selection have already been suggested in Chapter 6 but if there were a single principle on which to base assessment selection it would be *fitness for purpose*. This principle would, of course, have to be applied both to any general issues arising from the model and to the constituent parts of the proposed profile. As far as this book is concerned, these may be summarised as follows:

General Issues for Assessment for each Part of the Profile	Constituent Parts of the Profile
(1) Positive achievement	(1) Subject assessments
(2) Progression from the bottom up	(2) Cross-curricular skills
(3) Informal and in-course assessment	(3) Personal and social skills
(4) Wider involvement in assessment	(4) Achievements and experiences

'Fitness for purpose' has three particularly important practical implications for assessment.

(1) *It requires specific criteria to be translated into teaching/learning and assessment practices.* The key issue in assessment based upon specified criteria is how to translate the criteria into practice. What, for example, does 'Communicate effectively and appropriately in spoken English' (GCSE Subject Criteria in English 2.1.8) mean in terms of course and assessment design for a two-year course or a one-term module in English? What would 'Communicate effectively and appropriately' mean in, say, Physics, Home Economics, Music or Craft, Design and Technology, if the concern lay not with English but with communication across the curriculum? Only when criteria come to life in terms of teaching and learning can they be evaluated.

(2) *It underlines the importance of doing your thinking at the start in order to ensure that in assessment you do what you do by design and not by accident.* In teaching, a careful balance must always be struck between too much and too little involvement by the teacher and between the use of too rigid and too loose a set of objectives. Assessment has, however, to be concerned predominantly with output and not input and if it is to be fit for its purpose then this will have to be clarified in advance. Only then can one implement an assessment programme which will ensure that

(a) questions are asked and problems posed which will elicit relevant and appropriate evidence of positive performance

(b) there is a supportive and friendly environment within which assessment can take place.

(3) *It draws attention to the dangers of over-assessment.* One of the great dangers of assessment is *overkill* – the 'if it moves assess it' syndrome. Assessment should never become simply a trawling expedition in the hope of catching something. It must always have a clearly understood purpose. Over-assessment usually results from a failure to look at total programmes. We should therefore constantly be asking questions such as

(a) Do we need this information? and

(b) Have we already got sufficient information about this or that particular area or aspect?

We need to remember also that British experience in assessing the four constituent parts of the proposed profile is very uneven and we must take this into account in the preparation of training.

Subjects, for example, are what the British examination system and the British secondary school teacher knows best and feels most confident about assessing. Unfortunately, subjects have often been interpreted narrowly and this has resulted in assessment that is limited both in context and in method.There is, for instance, far too much stress upon terminal, written testing. The individual is emphasised at the expense of the group, and marks and grades are used as the sole form of feedback. The resulting patterns of assessment consequently fail to match up to the proposed model.

There is also considerable experience in schools of assessing achievements and experiences but this has usually taken the form of reports or references which have a fairly restricted view of what might be called an achievement or an experience. Students are rarely involved in the compilation and design of such documents. So far, in the area of achievements and experiences, little use has been made of descriptive assessment against pre-specified but mutually agreed criteria or of verification of what has actually occured by the person best able to provide it – who may not be a member of the school staff.

On the other hand there is very little assessment experience, particularly in the secondary school, of assessing cross-curricular skills; the track record of cross-curricular or integrated initiatives within the curriculum is a melancholy one, as the continuing debate on the nature of science for all and the difficulties encountered in implementing language across the curriculum indicate. Again, attitudes are the main problem and until we start to question outrageous assumptions like 'General Science is for those who cannot learn Physics, Chemistry, etc.' we will get nowhere. The only large-scale attempt to date to assess and certificate cross-curricular skills took place in Scotland and is described in *Pupils in Profile* (1977). It was particularly interesting in this study to see how the nature of certain subjects, for example, Home Economics, appeared to make it easier for those who taught them to assess across the curriculum.

There has also been relatively little formal experience of assessing personal and social skills. Dockrell and Black (1978), however, point out in their work on *Assessment in the Affective Domain* that this is done informally all the time and important judgements based on such assessment are often made. Assessment in this area also raises the issue of the role of the teacher as assessor more starkly than any other and it is particularly important that the kind of safeguards referred to in the Personal and Social Skills section of Chapter 6 are routinely implemented. It is also very important to recognise the ephemeral nature of much of the evidence and hence of most of the judgements made in this area.

Current practices therefore present us with two problems

uneven experience, confidence and expertise, and

the use of inappropriate assessment methods, timing and re-porting practices in those areas where we have experience.

Above all, there has been little attempt to involve the students themselves in the assessment process. All these factors will need to be taken into account when planning appropriate in-service training.

ASSESSMENT METHODS – SOME ISSUES

The remainder of this chapter will look at the following five issues relating to assessment methods.

(1) Asking the 'right' question

(2) Assignments and log books

(3) Descriptive assessment

(4) Observation

(5) Evaluating responses

In a book of this length, much will inevitably be left out and only those issues which seem most pertinent to the proposed assessment model and the constituent parts of the profile can be dealt with. Although suggestions will be made occasionally about using particular methods for particular parts of the profile, this does not mean that they are the only possibilities. Whether something is appropriate or inappropriate in any given situation must be a matter for judgement by those operating the profile. The proposed issues are also interconnected and their separation and order are purely matters of convenience.

1. Asking the 'right' question

This is a specific illustration of 'do what you do by design and not by accident'. The word 'question' is also shorthand for anything which requires the student to respond – whether in writing, orally or by doing something, thinking, making, playing, etc. Many of the questions we ask and the problems we pose are inappropriate because we do not give enough thought in advance to what we want to find out. It is perfectly reasonable for students to reply 'thick fog' in answer to the question 'The Battle of Hastings took place in ...?' Instead of blaming them for a stupid answer, we should blame ourselves for failing to word the question so as to obtain the answer we wanted, in this case, a date or a year. This is a frivolous example but far too much of our questioning makes it impossible to be sure whether an inability to answer is due to not knowing the answer or to a failure to understand what was asked. In the classroom, inappropriate questions can be asked again in a different way; in a formal assessment situation we have to live with those we have set. In order to avoid this, it is necessary to ask and answer two questions about every question we use.

(1) *What makes it difficult?* There are four elements in question difficulty: what is being assessed (information, concept or skill), format, content and accompanying material. The aim must be to ensure that the bulk of the difficulty arises from what is being assessed and that the other elements are kept as simple as possible.

(2) *What is its purpose?* A question can have many purposes. Is it, for example, to investigate the comprehensibility of a piece of material? Is it to direct the student's attention to something more significant or to lead in to a more searching question? Is it to provide evidence about students in terms of their understand-ing, knowledge, skills or attitudes? We need to be sure what our purposes are when considering what we are going to ask and not after we have received the answers.

Clarification of intent is, however, not the only reason for asking the 'right' question. We must also consider the extent to which a particular question can or cannot assess what we want it to assess. This is a particularly important issue when assessing skills, since it is neither possible nor desirable to set a specific question which tests a specific skill, largely because skills have more than one dimension. (This is also true of attitudes.) Comprehension, for example, includes inference and evaluation. It is therefore better to ask questions which involve problems or dilemmas and require decisions as to what are the most appropriate skills to use. The range of skills which can sensibly be selected can be controlled by the wording of the question or the dimensions of the problem. If these kinds of question are used, you must carefully consider, when setting them, how to evaluate the resulting answers. Setting questions and evaluating answers must be integrated although they are dealt with separately in this chapter.

Asking the 'right' question is a significant issue in all assessment, but it is likely to be particularly important in subject assessments and, to a lesser degree, with cross-curricular skills. Asking the 'right' question is also a crucial classroom skill and the more skilled a teacher is at this, the more the student will learn. From time to time, therefore, individuals, departments and whole institutions need to scrutinise the questions they ask in the classroom and by way of formal assessment by asking such things as :

(1) Given the abilities and interest of the pupil and the nature of the course, what different kinds of answer would I anticipate by way of response?

(2) Did I actually get the kinds of answer I anticipated?

(3) What is the weakest answer which would show a worthwhile level of response?

(4) Could the point of the question be made more apparent to the students without restricting the range of responses – for example, by constructing the question round a fallacy or a dilemma?

Such a process can only improve the quality of questions and this in its turn must improve the quality of the answers.

2. Assignments and log books

Assignments

An assignment is a task or a problem given to individuals or groups of students to undertake or resolve. These tasks should be sharply focused against detailed sets of specific criteria and may consist of a chain of related tasks or a number of self-contained ones. Within subject assessments, the graded French and German test programmes developed by Graded Objectives for Achievement in Language Skills (GOALS) or by the Kent Mathematics Project provide examples of a chain of related tasks. The seven assignments which constitute the two-year coursework programme for History 13–16 are a good example of self-contained tasks. Assignments stand in the middle of the assessment spectrum between formal terminal examinations on the one hand and continuous assessment on the other. Their potential for use in profiles is very considerable and has not yet been fully exploited. Assignments possess five prominent features.

(1) *They can readily be made cross-curricular in scope.* One problem facing teachers embarking on profiles in schools is how to expand the subject environment and widen the contexts of teaching. We often talk about 'the mathematics or science of the high street' or 'communication in everyday life' but do very little to develop these concepts in practice. Appropriately designed and exploited assignments have considerable potential for breaking down subject barriers.

(2) *They can make very specific demands on students and can in consequence be very practical and task-oriented.* This has disadvantages as well as advantages. Many assignments currently involve social and vocational skills, where the need to be practical and use 'real' activities is paramount. This has caused some who ought to know better to suggest that assignments as a learning and assessment tool have only limited relevance. More work must therefore be done to develop assignments exploiting criteria running right across the curriculum.

(3) *They lend themselves to – and indeed encourage – group work, which is almost totally ignored in assessment, particularly in public examinations.* A well-planned course involving a range of assignments which pose different challenges but collectively cover a complete set of criteria can provide ample opportunities for all students to demonstrate what they can do right across the board. It can also provide an ideal framework upon which an employer can place his or her own template of requirements.

(4) *They provide a good vehicle for involving students both in their own learning and in their own assessment.* The nature of an assignment can be discussed and determined in advance between teacher and student, and they will provide many opportunities for self-evaluation, particularly when used in conjunction with a log book or where group work is involved. Assignments – particularly those which are work based – also enable a much wider range of people to be involved in their development and assessment. They can thus help to bridge the artificial and damaging gaps which still exist all too frequently between education and training and between the workplace and the classroom.

(5) *They encourage progression and lend themselves particularly well to the assessment of individual programmes based on a set of common criteria* – thus permitting all students to demonstrate what they know, understand and can do. Assignments are therefore particularly appropriate for the assessment model proposed at the beginning of this chapter and the constituent parts of the profile. They are particularly relevant to cross-curricular and social and vocational skills but are also extremely useful for subject assessment and as a basis for demonstrating achievements outside the formal curriculum.

The main challenge facing anyone wishing to use assignments is to ensure that the tasks and problems proposed are appropriate. This is just like the issue raised in the section on setting the 'right' question and requires teacher and student to translate their objectives, purposes or criteria, however expressed, into assignments which will constitute suitable vehicles for continuous interactive learning. The challenge is a demanding one but the rewards are enormous.

Log Books

Log books have been used almost exclusively to date as part of the record-keeping process in profiles related to pre-vocational courses such as CGLI 365. A log book is like a diary in which the student regularly notes what has been experienced and learned in relation to specific elements of a course. It thus forms the basis for regular reviews of progress. Less use has been made of the log book as a specific part of the assessment but it can provide a very powerful tool for student self-evaluation and external assessment either on its own or in association with other pieces of work. The skills needed for maintaining and using log books must incidentally be developed and assessed as part of the course programme.

Another profiling use for log books concerns the choice of suitable assignments. If criteria are successfully matched with specific teaching and learning strategies students will be presented with challenges in the form of questions, problems and assignments which let them show whether or not they can meet the criteria. This emphasises once again the importance of asking the right question. Assignments present a particular difficulty here because they involve work spread over several days or even weeks. Although the actions taken by students to overcome problems resulting from a poor assignment can provide useful learning experiences, it is important that every effort is made to set appropriate assignments. One way of doing this is for the teacher to note in a log book the reasons for the choice of an assignment and its anticipated outcomes at the time the decision is taken. When this information is compared with that recorded in the log book about the problems of implementation and the eventual results the teacher has an extremely useful aide memoire for selecting future assignments.

One potential advantage of both assignments and log books is their contribution to promoting and measuring progression. The need to do this is absolutely central to the positive use of assessment for diagnosis and guidance and for the development of systems of credit accumulation and credit transfer. Assignments used in conjunction with log books can often provide a more effective way of measuring progression than graded tests, but this will of course depend on the nature of the criteria being assessed and the extent to which genuine progression in a developmental sense can be justified. Unfortunately, we know far too little about how young people think to be anything but cautious about this.

3. Descriptive assessment

Descriptive assessment means just what it says. Most of the current methods used to describe performance, such as grades and marks, are extremely uninformative. We therefore tend to provide descriptions of performance in reports or references which mainly make their judgements by omission and are not intended for diagnostic use. What we need and lack are annotated descriptions, which can bridge the gap between reporting and assessing. The main use of such descriptions should be internal and therefore for students and teachers but they can also be used to provide information about performance to parents and employers. Descriptive assessment is, in a sense, a mini-profile within a relatively restricted area.

A number of profiles in this country have made or are currently making use of descriptive assessment in this way. The illustration overleaf comes from the Sutton Centre, Nottinghamshire, and relates to Literature and Drama.

One of the featues of this particular approach is the opportunity that it provides for comments by both parent and student. A much fuller version linked to work requirements and assessment criteria has been developed by VISE as part of its assessment programme for Years 11 and 12 (the last two years of full-time secondary education). As a result of its work in this area, VISE has developed and published an extremely useful set of guidelines for both the use and the writing of descriptive assessments. Much of what follows in the rest of this section has drawn heavily from this experience.

The guidelines for use with their reference to explicit assessment criteria, student participation and feedback built upon positive achievement very much mirror the model for assessment suggested at the beginning of this chapter. They stress three important characteristics of assessment not yet mentioned but which ought to feature in any overall profiling programme.

Teacher's Comments

D's work is spoilt by her spelling and her inability to

give work in to be marked when it is finished. She is

imaginative but must organise herself to finish work and

take pride in it. It has taken her a long time to

settle down at the Centre and I am sure she will soon be

forging ahead!

Signed

Pupil's Comments

15th July

I agree with this coment. My spelling is bad I will try

and improve it. This term in lit and drama has been

quite interesting.

Signed

Parent's Comments

D has been given a dictionary to help improve her

spelling, she will be encouraged to use it and to be

prompt in handing in finished work.

Signed

(1) *It should be natural and not contrived.* Too much of our current assessment in secondary schools is 'whitewashing' for the external moderator and this often leads to totally unnecessary assessment being undertaken.

(2) *It should achieve continuity* and thus enable students to see each assessment in relation to what has gone before and as preparation for what is to follow.

(3) *It should not be dogmatic* in presuming to provide the only answer.

The guidelines suggested for writing descriptive assessments are particularly pertinent for profiling because they are specifically intended for reporting within a subject frame of reference. They include the following suggestions.

Achievements should be reported in terms of the qualities demonstrated as well as in relation to criteria.

Evidence should always be provided to support statements or judgements.

Descriptions should be work-based and describe what the student has achieved.

They should be fair, relevant, accurate and adequate.

What does a descriptive assessment based on these guidelines look like? Two examples follow taken from the *Guidelines for Descriptive Assessment* (VISE 1985). The first relates to performance at the end of a three-unit course in the Creative Arts and the second to performance in a single unit in an English course. Comments are provided in both cases and draw attention to the satisfactory features of the first and the unsatisfactory features of the second as reports.

You might like to compare these two descriptive assessments with the annotated VISE report for Marta given on page 39. This is written in a much more structured form for a student who is at an earlier stage of her schooling (Year 8) than Anna and Marilyn. The prime concern therefore in Marta's case is satisfactory completion of a stage in a course as a basis for proceeding to the next stage and this is clearly more important for her than it is for Marilyn. It is thus very much a formative document whereas the other two, particularly Anna's, are beginning to make more summative statements.

CREATIVE ARTS

(3 UNITS)   ANNA

completion
of the work is
described in
qualitative
terms

→ Anna successfully completed the requirements of the course including course negotiation.***

Anna's journal was a detailed description of her involvement in Creative Arts. In the journal she explained the planning, preparation, and development of each folio piece. Her self-evaluation statement perceptively described the strengths and weaknesses of her folio. Her on-going evaluation provided the means to develop further the directions of her folio.***

judgements
of the
← student are
backed by
evidence

details of
the work
completed

→ Anna's folio contained a considerable quantity of work, and included tasks undertaken both at school and in evening printmaking classes. All her work was imaginative and technically competent. Anna studied printmaking, completing a folio of etchings, both dry point and aquatint; silk-screen printing using profilm and block-out; wood-cuts and lino cuts. She studied and controlled technique, used colour and form appropriately and carefully mounted major pieces.***

Anna worked co-operatively with other students and contributed to group tasks, such as the school mural.***

End of statement

- This report describes the qualities of achievements in addition to detailing the work completed.

- Satisfactory completion of the course is by completing work in an agreed way. In this type of report a view of the student's relationship to the work emerges, along with an account of the work completed.

- This type of report can be difficult to write well; there is a tendency to lapse into value-laden judgements of the student's character or speculation about the student's ability, while the report should be restricted to a description of the student's achievements in the work completed.

ENGLISH

(1 UNIT)   MARILYN

an
unnecessarily →
negative
beginning to
an account of
a term's work

Marilyn's written expression continues to
reveal weaknesses. Her film review was disjointed
and unstructured, failing to elaborate a central
idea into a coherent whole. She used awkward
syntax and failed totally to support any of her
judgements with detail from the film. She has not   ← an analysis of
really grasped the techniques of analysis or   work done is
criticism.***   clearly
                                                            relevant for
why not say
'she
contributed
to class
discussion
although ...'

Her descriptive pieces lacked structure and   the student to
depth, although they exhibit fewer grammatical or   improve but
spelling errors. In place of her autobiography, she   expressions
completed a short story which, although based   like 'fails
rather closely on one we had read in class,   totally' and
nevertheless showed care and effort. Her   'has not really
→ contribution in class discussion remained fairly   grasped' are
sporadic, although it is plain that she   listened   extreme

dangerous →
speculation

carefully, her comprehension of finer details and   statements
subtle differences is lacking.***   that
                                                          discourage

this would be a →
more positive
beginning to
the report

Her attitude, attendance and completion of her
contracts for the term earned her the second unit   rather than
in English.***   encourage
                                                          improvement
End of statement

- An unsympathetic report of a student's work. It concentrates on the weaknesses rather than the strengths of the work completed.

- A reader might be surprised that the student's work in the unit was satisfactory after reading the details of the report.

- A more detailed elaboration of the criteria for success and the work completed are essential.

- This report is clearly unstructured and not written to a predetermined plan and so speculation and random evaluations dominate the report.

4. Observation

Frequent reference has been made in earlier chapters to the importance of informal observation in assessing a wide range of skills and activities likely to play an important part in profiles. Unfortunately, comparatively little work seems to have been carried out on developing the relevant skills of observation in teachers and students. Considerable emphasis has been placed upon classroom observation skills for student teachers; the APU has undertaken work, particularly in Science, on the development of tasks requiring observation by students. There has also been the occasional teacher, like John Miller of the Blakelaw School, Newcastle, who has made use of observation as a basis for improving learning. He used videos of classroom activities in relation to group discussion within a humanities curriculum (Dale and Elliott, 1972 – see page 141). There is also growing awareness of the importance of observation of classroom performance as a part of teacher appraisal.

What, however, has been lacking is work on observation by the teacher and indeed the student as a basis for student assessment. This is surprising because teachers are constantly assessing their students informally and making intuitive and unstructured use of a multitude of signs both verbal and non-verbal through which skills, attitudes, knowledge and understanding are revealed. What is needed is to use this observation consciously and selectively to assess in a structured rather than ad hoc fashion. Such assessment could of course take place both inside and outside the classroom.

The use of observation as a basis for assessment could be particularly useful in tasks involving practical and oral skills and in relation to qualities and attitudes. We need to know what students can do as well as what they are disposed to do. Observation schedules are one way of achieving this. They can be used both as a basis for student assessment and as a means of improving teacher and student skills. In both cases they would act as a kind of checklist. Parts of two teacher–produced inventories for Arithmetic and Personal and Social Skills (see opposite) illustrate both their format and their problems. They appear in full in the Open University/Schools Council Course booklet on *Measuring Learning Outcomes* (1981) which formed part of the 'Curriculum in Action: An Approach to Evaluation' course.

Arithmetic

Checklist	Completed		
	1st Year	2nd Year	3rd Year
Name: _____			
1. Knows cardinal numbers and can count number of objects in a set			
2. Knows, can write and understand written numerals			
3. Knows and understands ordinal numbers 1st, 2nd, 3rd, etc.			
4. Knows terms, big, small, different, biggest, smallest, more, less, matches, many, few, longest, shortest, set, sets			
5. Can recognise coins 1p, 2p, 5p, 10p, 50p			
6. Has concept of a set and members of a set (classifying, sorting, matching)			
7. Has concept of equality and inequality of sets. Understands a sub-set			
8. Knows terms, same, equal, straight, curved, tall, taller, tallest, long, longer, longest, balance, heavy, heavier, heaviest, greater, less, add			
9. Has concept of place value in base ten, e.g. 1 ten and 3 units			
10. Has concept of conservation of number			

Personal and Social Skills

What we are aiming for	Always	Usually	Seldom	Never	Sometimes
Name: _____					
1. Cooperates well with teacher					
2. Cooperates well with other pupils					
3. Shows interest in work					
4. Thinks for him/herself					
5. Is keen to get on with work					
6. Contributes to group discussions					
7. Works consistently and is not easily distracted					
8. Does independent reading					
9. Has good recall of knowledge					
10. Is efficient at finding out information					

The Arithmetic inventory is reasonably clear about what is being assessed although some of the items would have been better if they had been broken up into a series of discrete parts as in item 4. Categorical decisions such as the 'yes/no' used here do not suit certain of the items, for example, numbers 4, 6, 7, 8, 9, 10, and some of the terminology is vague. What does one record, for instance, for a student who knows some but not 'all' of the terms in item 8? At what point is a concept grasped?

The Personal and Social Skills inventory is inevitably vague on occasions and the descriptions need to be more closely related to specific tasks. It is also very much related to age and the standards of judgement will inevitably change with age.

Professionally developed inventories of the kind which Wynne Harlen and others produced in *Match and Mismatch* (1977) avoid many of these basic faults. They are therefore extremely useful tools for diagnosis, guidance and evaluation, in this case in relation to student development in primary science. For maximum value such inventories must concentrate upon what is observable in student behaviour and relate to a planned series of learning experiences. If they do this they can make teachers more sensitive to those student qualities which are significant in specific contexts and offer a systematic alternative to formal testing. They are particularly useful for the assessment of personal and social development and qualities which are not easily tested by normal methods. They need not be obtrusive although they are susceptible to personal interpretation and hence to the halo effect*. Their main potential for profiling does not, however, lie in their increased use as part of the assessment package itself but as a means of training teachers to be more perceptive and systematic in observation and thus able to create a less stressful and more open environment. There is a wide variety of observational experience already available in schools, and the Drama department, for example, may well have skills in observation

---

*The term 'halo effect' describes a bias in assessment arising from the tendency of the assessor to be influenced in his/her judgement of specifics by his/her general impression of the individual being assessed. It is in consequence important in relation to teacher assessment of their own students.

resulting from the nature of its work and the subject which could be of value to, say, Physics teachers, and vice versa. What is needed is to harness and increase this experience and inventories of the kind described offer one way of doing this.

Observation is a continuous process and when used for assessment it cannot realistically be judged or moderated by someone outside as is the case with more formal assessment. Only the person undertaking the assessment is in a position to make the necessary judgements. Continuous assessment of this kind is increasingly needed to meet criteria even in subject areas in public examinations such as oral and practical skills in GCSE English and Science. The only solution lies in *accreditation*. This is the process whereby a body – possibly established specifically for the purpose – grants, say, a certificate or a licence to other individuals or agencies to undertake activities on its behalf.

For example, an examining body can accredit a teacher to undertake assessment on its behalf and underwrites the resulting judgement, however expressed (for example, a grade, mark or a verbal statement), by issuing its certificate. Accreditation raises a number of very significant issues. Under what conditions? For how long? Should an individual, a department or an institution be accredited? What kind of training is or ought to be provided? In conjunction with validation referred to later in this chapter, it forms a possible basis for establishing the credibility of school profiles and for providing appropriate training for teachers, thus freeing them to develop programmes of work which completely integrate assessment.

5. Evaluating responses

Reference has already been made to the uninformative nature of both marks and grades whether they are used in a classroom or in a GCSE examination. If assessment is to provide the range of information needed for profiles of the kind outlined in this book, it must make use of more appropriate methods for describing student performance. This could be difficult when a profiling system incorporates public examination results but moves towards criterion referencing will help here. Various possible ways of improving the situation have already been suggested but four in particular will be dealt with here.

Annotation
Marking levels
Verification
Validation

Annotation and *marking levels* can probably be used to best advantage in *subject assessments and cross-curricular skills* where the criteria for assessment are most easily related to tasks. Considerable work has been undertaken in both these areas by the History 13–16 Project and some of this will be used by way of illustration. Other examples of levels have already been provided. (See in particular the CGLI basic abilities profile on pages 3–4.) *Verification* is a particularly useful approach for reporting *achievements and experiences. Validation* is concerned with approval of whole course structures and processes rather than the practical details.

Annotation

Annotation is a way of showing how and where previously agreed criteria have been met in a piece of work. Its value comes from the feedback it can provide. If well done, it provides an ideal basis for discussions between students and teachers about a piece of work whether it is being prepared or has been completed. The quality of such discussion can be further enhanced if the criteria themselves emerge from joint discussion between teachers and students. The work of John Miller in a course based on the Stenhouse Humanities Project referred to on page 99 provides a good example of such feedback.

Miller's objective was to improve the quality of group discussion. He created his teaching materials by videotaping classroom discussions involving about ten of his students. These videos were then played back to the students who were asked initially to record the number of comments each student had made. A high level of agreement was reached fairly quickly although it was necessary on occasion to agree what constituted a comment. (How about 'Ah ha', for example?) The students were then asked to evaluate the comments on a three-point scale against a single criterion upon which they had agreed, such as relevance to the topic under discussion. The number of criteria used and the length of the scale were then progressively extended until a workable matrix for assessing both group discussion and student performance emerged. Apart from being a useful exercise, the strategy used to create the matrix improved student perception of the requirements of group discussion, improved the quality of the discussion itself and made it easier to assess individual contributions. In short, it created a profile for group discussion through annotation.

A rather more common use of annotation is to be found in History 13–16. Here the coursework programme requires students to produce between five and seven assignments over a two-year period. Each of these pieces has to meet a stated general objective and a series of specific criteria. One of these assignments has as its general objective the 'Evaluation and Interpretation of Sources'. The eight specified criteria for meeting the objective include

Using one source to corroborate another
Relating sources to their historical context
Assessing the value of the sources as evidence for the historian

These criteria constitute the framework for teaching and learning and the teacher has to ensure, for example, that opportunities are provided in the classroom for cross-referencing between sources. The distinction between evidence and information has also to be clearly established and so on. The stated criteria form the basis for annotating the pieces of work produced by the students in relation to the overall objective and thus ensure feedback. If required, all the information resulting from annotation can be used to build up a diagnostic profile for the students either individually or collectively and/or for the assignments. What cannot be done is to use annotation to give a mark to a piece of work and hence a grade to a student. If this is a requirement then the possibility of devising marking levels against criteria needs to be looked at. This is the subject of the next section in relation to students only although it is important to recognise that you can grade the quality of assignments as end-products.

Marking Levels

There are two ways to devise marking levels.

(1) To concentrate on the *global objectives* and define levels of performance in relation to them.

(2) To break down the global objectives into the requirements for achieving them (knowledge skills, understanding, attitudes, etc.). These can be stated in terms of *specific criteria* and *levels of performance* developed in relation to them.

Method 1

Global objectives can be defined with various degrees of generality. John Miller's objective was to improve the quality of group discussion. The History 13–16 objective was the 'Evaluation and Interpretation of Sources'. An objective in Mathematics might be the mastery of quadratic equations.

An attempt to define a high-level and a low-level performance in relation to the History 13–16 global objective would probably result in something like this

Low-level performance
Able to extract information from the sources. Shows nothing more than comprehension of words or graphics and does not make any inferences going beyond the information given.

High-level performance
Able to extract from the source its meaning and its value as evidence for the historian as distinct from its surface value as information. Can compare, corroborate, detect omissions, etc. as appropriate so as to establish the value of the source with clarity and precision.

You might like to try and supply the description for a medium-level performance. One possible way of tightening up these descriptions would be to identify some general indicators of performance in relation to the objective, such as, for example, attributing sources properly, arguing logically, giving evidence of grasping general ideas and so on. As soon as one does this however one tends to stop looking at the global objective and starts instead to evaluate the work against the general indicators. Difficulties will of course increase with the number of levels used.

Method 2

This method is the one adopted in GCSE for grade-related criteria. In History, for example, there are three global objectives or *domains*.

(I) Historical knowledge and understanding

(II) Historical enquiry

(III) Historical reasoning

Each of these has three or four elements and each element is divided into four levels. This results in the following description for a Level 4 performance (the highest) for Element D (making a judgement) in Domain III: 'The student is able to reach a historically valid explanation supported by a process of cross-referencing'. This is followed by about ten lines of amplification. This approach certainly has the potential to improve our understanding of teaching and learning (in this case in history). It is less certain, however, whether it is likely to be more helpful diagnostically or for grading purposes than the high- and low-level descriptions provided above for a global objective.

Enough has now been said to reinforce the point made in Chapter 2 that there is a significant clash of interests between profiles which look *inward* to students and to teaching and learning and those which look *outward* to employers and selection. This tension is greatest when work is being marked and performance described. Internal usage needs a substantial amount of specific information which does not require comparisons to be made between one student and another. External usage needs much less information presented in ways which allow such comparisons. Marking levels can provide a possible way of bridging this gap. The resulting grid-style profiles are, however, subject to the kinds of criticism made in the Scottish Vocational Preparation Unit's publication *Made to Measure?* (1982), that is, over-generalised descriptions and uneven gaps between levels. We may never be able to avoid degrading information by reducing and collapsing it but we must continue to try and find approaches which reduce this tension. Unless we can do this there is going to be a constant problem about the practical use of profiles.

Marking levels and annotation have, however, some real advantages for internal use in profiling.

(1) They provide information as a basis for student/teacher discussion.
(2) They have a built-in requirement for analysis particularly where subject assessment and cross-curricular skills are involved.
(3) The use of levels results in a bottom-up model* for assessment.

Verification and validation in different ways provide possible solutions to the problem of the clash of interests between inward-looking and outward-looking profiles. *Verification* suggests a means of presenting information which is useful but not competitive in the sense that grades are. *Validation* suggests a mechanism for establishing the credibility of a profile at least at the local level.

Verification

This means that statements made on a report, record or any other document are verified or signed as correct by the person who is most able to do this. By the signature, the person concerned implies his or her willingness to confirm the statement. This verification could be provided by the Associated Board of the Royal School of Music's Grade IV in the Flute, or by the Department of Transport driving licence or by the local supermarket manager, scoutmaster or clergyman. No value judgement is given; that is supplied by anyone reading it. It is simply the accuracy of the statement that is being underwritten. For example, the fact that I sing bass in the church

---

*Bottom-up assessment starts by asking what is the lowest level of rewardable response and builds up from the bottom. It thus facilitates progression and the assessment of positive achievement for all students. It is usually contrasted with top-down assessment, where the concern lies with the best performance and where the achievement of others is compared with this, usually to their disadvantage. A 'levels' mark scheme will facilitate bottom-up assessment whereas a model answer marking scheme leads to top-down. Any shift from norm to criterion referencing requires a shift from a top-down to a bottom-up model of assessment, and this is implicit in much of what has been said in this chapter.

choir does not suggest how well I sing nor whether I am a regular attender at choir practice unless I choose to say that I sing well and am a regular attender.

Verification can be particularly useful in relation to achievements and experiences. It provides the opportunity for the students to control what they want to say about themselves. This part of a profile can be entirely student-initiated and operated although it is perfectly possible to provide a set of headings under which achievements and experiences can be listed. It also has the merit of increasing the range of those involved in the profiling process since many of those who will be asked to verify statements will not be teachers. Involvement is by far the best way of developing interest, increasing understanding, and establishing credibility. It is also possible to extend verification to all reports about students by making it an obligatory feature of a profile that the student signs a report as a fair and, where appropriate, accurate statement.

Validation

Validation is not a new process in education but is one which has been little used in the context of school assessment. It is the process whereby approval is given to arrangements for the development of courses of study and their related assessment in accordance with an agreed set of rules. It is concerned with overall programmes and not with the nuts and bolts through which such programmes are re-alised. Tyrell Burgess and Betty Adams in Outcomes of Education (1980) proposed that all schools should establish external validating bodies to review the process by which students planned their programmes. It would therefore be the main purpose of such boards to see that the arrangements made by schools for the negotiation of learning were consistent and working as intended. Such boards are particularly suitable for institutional profile schemes particularly those involving schools within a single local authority. One of the DES-funded pilot schemes, the Dorset/Southern Regional Exam-ination Board (SREB) Assessment and Profiling Project is setting up school validation boards to monitor its development and operation. The membership of each board will consist of represen-tatives from the governors, the LEA, the SREB, another school, parents, employers and staff. Consideration is also being given to having student representation. The effectiveness of these boards and in particular their influence on establishing credibility locally will form part of the overall evaluation of the project. This is very important for the long term success of profiles that focus on the development and recognition of individual students' achievement and its relationship to the whole of what goes on within an institution and the community it serves, both formal and informal. This is of course what this book advocates and it is at the heart of the Dorset/SREB Project. Currently, successful delivery of the formal curriculum largely takes place through public examinations and their results, particularly for students between the ages of 14 and 19. If profiles are to establish credibility they must be seen as valid alternatives to public examinations and not simply as extensions to them.

You may think that this chapter has not dealt properly with the assessment of personal and social skills. This is the most difficult and contentious of the four constituent parts of the suggested profile because of the changing nature of the demands placed on young people by society and the effects of growing maturity. The kinds of schedule suggested above in the section on observation can be used for assessing such skills and can be tailored for the purpose. You can also use verification and comment banks but these can be extremely artificial and restrictive. Much of the information on personal and social skills is likely to result either

directly from student self-assessment which the whole ethos of a profile can encourage, or

indirectly from carefully thought-out tasks which do not have personal and social skills among their overtly stated criteria particularly when the tasks involve group work. As Dockrell and Black (1980) remind us, we also need to try and clarify what having a particular attribute or quality actually means in practical terms within a school curriculum. This whole area too often lacks definition and so the means to generate information are also lacking.

None of the assessment methods described or suggested in this chapter can operate without the wholehearted co-operation and support of all who teach and learn in the institution where profiles are operated. Assessment constitutes the hub around which all aspects of a profile revolve and it should not be regarded as something separate from the normal day-to-day business of teaching and learning. This chapter therefore closes as it opened by emphasising the importance of changing attitudes as an essential prerequisite for success.

Chapter 8

IMPLICATIONS FOR THE INSTITUTION

If a scheme of profile assessment is to be introduced somewhere where there is little appreciation of its possible implications for the institution's organisation and structure, then there is little chance of its success or there are likely to be, at least, significant operational difficulties. This is especially so where a profiling system is tied closely to the curriculum. You must therefore try to anticipate the effects on the institution before the scheme is formally introduced and plan strategies for change.

Where a school or college designs and implements its own scheme of profile assessment there are likely to be profound changes in many areas of organisation such as

Curriculum
Pastoral organisation and guidance systems
Recording and reporting systems
Assessment policies
Staff-development programmes

The implications are substantial. Learners, teachers and users will all be affected. All this change must be managed, structured and paced. The introduction of a scheme of profile assessment can, however, provide the basis for planned school review, reappraisal and staff development.

At the heart of the teaching process there will be other changes concerning teaching methods and learning styles. These will occur differently in various classrooms but it is inevitable that a process which attempts to discover student progress and achievements in response to specified curriculum objectives will lead to a more individualised learning process.

You will not be surprised to discover that introducing profiling will also affect assessment practices and the programmes required to develop teachers' skills in assessment techniques and recording methods. Review and reappraisal are likely to result in the following areas

Curriculum
Pastoral and guidance systems
Recording and reporting systems

We hope that we have already made sufficient suggestions about possible changes in assessment practices and that it is evident by now that you will need to organise staff-development programmes to implement change in these three areas and in relation to assessment.

IMPLICATIONS FOR THE CURRICULUM

One of our main arguments has been that curriculum and assessment objectives should be planned, developed and evaluated jointly. This is a major thrust which will take years to evolve. This strategy must also be flexible enough to respond to national curriculum and assessment initiatives and to local and institutional needs. The benefits of this approach cannot, however, be over-stated. The joint planning of curriculum and assessment objectives will lead to large-scale improvement in the quality of the education provided because it will unify the total educational experience for everyone concerned. A student or teacher will get little help from a profile which does not emerge from curriculum discussions and joint planning of curriculum and assessment. A profile which emerges without a thorough review and reappraisal of the curriculum is only likely to reflect imperfect curriculum provision and practices.

The starting point for this joint planning is unimportant. There are many teachers who believe that profiles should be influenced by the curriculum, but in practice many are led to curriculum development through a consideration of assessment policies. Sometimes the learning experience clearly identifies the assessment objectives, but sometimes curriculum opportunities need to be designed so that specific skills, attitudes or concepts can be assessed.

There are other ways in which assessment can assist curriculum planning. Assessment is usually seen in relation to the individual: *what is the response of the student to the learning experience provided by the institution?*

This is its main purpose. But it is also important for evaluating the success of the curriculum objectives in terms of achieving the declared aims of the institution. There can be no effective evaluation of the curriculum without a structured assessment programme which selects the most appropriate assessment techniques to achieve a particular aim. In this way the profile can provide a focus for inter-departmental discussion on the total curriculum provision of the institution.

For the teacher, assessment is important for evaluating how successful the teaching programme has been in allowing students to achieve specific aims and objectives. The assessment may provide information about the suitability of the content, the pace of the work, the degree of difficulty, the teaching methods used and the materials.

How can curriculum and assessment objectives be planned jointly in practice? It is important to devise a plan to do this and highlight the stages of development which might require external support. The following outline specification from *Curriculum 11–16: Towards a Statement of Entitlement* might be useful for designing an approach to the problem.

2. An outline specification

The work of the enquiry has led to the conclusion that any adequate specification of the curriculum to which all pupils are entitled up to 16 should include . . . :

i   a statement of aims relating to the education of the individuals and to the preparation of young people for life after school;

ii   a statement of objectives in terms of skills, attitudes, concepts and knowledge;

iii   a balanced allocation of time for all the eight areas of experience (the aesthetic and creative; the ethical; the linguistic; the mathematical; the physical; the scientific; the social and political; and the spiritual) which reflects the importance of each and a judgement of how various component courses contribute to these areas;

iv provision for the entitlement curriculum in all five years for all pupils of 70–80 per cent of the time available with the remaining time for various other components to be taken by pupils according to their individual talents and interests;

v methods of teaching and learning which ensure the progressive acquisition by pupils of the desired skills, attitudes, concepts and knowledge;

vi a policy for staffing and resource allocation which is based on the curriculum;

vii acceptance of the need for assessment which monitors pupils' progress in learning, and for explicit procedures, accessible to the public, which reflect and reinforce i. to v. above.

Designing institutional aims

It is hardly surprising that most students do not realise that a single educational experience is provided in the differing packages put before them; most teachers – particularly in schools – do not really see the curriculum in any unified sense. There is therefore no direction to the whole educational experience, even though departmental contributions may be effective, stimulating and coherent. In short, the institution becomes rudderless.

Before there can be any educational planning a set of school aims must be developed and accepted by the staff. Education is more likely to be provided successfully when all the staff are actively pursuing and promoting the same educational aims and carefully structuring curriculum objectives in each area to achieve those aims. Aims should not be part of the prospectus quickly flicked through by parents and teachers alike nor statements picked out of a hat after the course has been planned.

If the LEA has published its own curriculum policy statement, it would be logical to use its aims as a focus for discussion and a framework for the institutional aims. College teachers will need to interpret the aims of national courses into their own terms. It is better to have a limited number of aims which can be accepted by everyone rather than a long list which is either too cumbersome to allow agreement or too detailed to be a common focus. The aims should be compatible, harmonious and achievable.

If the LEA has not published a curriculum policy statement it may be useful to focus discussions on a set of aims from national documents. Outlined below are aims from *The School Curriculum*, DES, 1981, and the Warnock Report *Special Education Needs*, DES, 1978.

' . . . first, to enlarge a child's knowledge, experience and imaginative understanding and thus his awareness of moral values and capacity for enjoyment; and secondly, to enable him to enter the world after formal education is over as an active participant in society and a responsible contributor to it, capable of achieving as much independence as possible.'

Special Education Needs

'(1) to help pupils to develop lively, enquiring minds, the ability to question and argue rationally and to apply themselves to tasks, and physical skills;
(2) to help pupils to acquire knowledge and skills relevant to adult life and employment in a fast-changing world;
(3) to help pupils to use language and number effectively;
(4) to instil respect for religious and moral values, and tolerance of other races, religions and ways of life;
(5) to help pupils to understand the world in which they live, and the interdependence of individuals, groups and nations;
(6) to help pupils to appreciate human achievements and aspirations.'

The School Curriculum

What have such aims to do with profiling? They are critically important and should determine the curriculum of the school. The assessment objectives should help the school to achieve these aims because they enable evaluation of the curriculum to be carried through effectively and the assessment methods should fulfil the aims.

Translating aims into practice

Translating aims into curriculum objectives is not an easy task and often curriculum content does not actively promote the achievement of the declared aims. This is because too often the curriculum is seen as a collection of separate, unrelated components rather than as a unified curriculum experience for the student. In curriculum planning there must be less emphasis on input and more on what the student takes away.

'To teach each subject without close reference to others, or to an overall framework of educational objectives, is to risk losing that very breadth and "wholeness" which most schools, in their aims, undertake to provide. Important skills, for example the ability to draw upon information from a variety of sources to help solve a problem, may be substantially neglected; and the opportunity for knowledge and insight gained in one subject to be reinforced in another may not be taken.'

The Curriculum from 5 to 16 Curriculum Matters 2
HMI Series,1985

One way to tackle the problem is to define curriculum objectives in terms of skills, attitudes, concepts and knowledge.

But before this can be done the teachers must be aware of the institutional aims so that they remain central to the development of the curriculum objectives, and they must agree on a working definition for the terms they intend or are likely to use.

Curriculum objectives may then be devised in a number of ways, described below.

Discussion of an Existing Model

You may decide that an existing model of curriculum objectives should be discussed by the entire staff and in departments. Such models may be found in LEA curriculum policy statements or in *Curriculum 11–16: Towards a Statement of Entitlement.* Such discussions could identify specific objectives for achieving individual institutional aims and specific and general departmental objectives. These could then be recorded within a grid format to reveal any duplication and omissions and further discussion would produce the detail of direct curriculum design.

Independent Departmental Discussion

Members of each department could discuss the objectives which should be devised to develop the institutional aims. All the departments' objectives could then be collated into a grid format such as the one shown overleaf as a focus for discussion by the whole staff. This would lead to further review and reappraisal and should result in a statement of curriculum objectives.

SKILLS

Subject	Aesthetic	Oral	Study	Graphic	Physical	Written	Cognitive	Numerical	Reading	Aural
Lang	•	•	•	•	•	•	•	•	•	•
Art	•	•	•	•	•	•	•	•	•	•
Home Ec	•	•	•	•	•	•	•	•	•	•
Tech	•	•	•	•	•	•	•	•	•	•
History	•	•	•	•	•	•	•	•	•	•
Geog	•	•	•	•	•	•	•	•	•	•
Soc St	•	•	•	•	•	•	•	•	•	•
English	•	•	•	•	•	•	•	•	•	•
Biology	•	•	•	•	•	•	•	•	•	•
Chem	•	•	•	•	•	•	•	•	•	•
Physics	•	•	•	•	•	•	•	•	•	•
Drama	•	•	•	•	•	•	•	•	•	•
Maths	•	•	•	•	•	•	•	•	•	•
Rem	•	•	•	•	•	•	•	•	•	•
P.E.	•	•	•	•	•	•	•	•	•	•
Careers	•	•	•	•	•	•	•	•	•	•
Music	•	•	•	•	•	•	•	•	•	•

Whether you choose discussion of an existing model or independent departmental discussion, the process is likely to be an extended one with further discussion, redrafting and review until agreement is reached.

Use of an Objectives Board Game
You might find this useful to focus discussion at both departmental and inter-departmental level.

You will need three sets of ten cards each measuring 10 cm by 4 cm. One colour is used to identify each set of cards (*Skills, Attitudes* or *Concepts*) and the following thirty objectives are written on them.

Objectives Board Game Cards

Skills	Attitudes	Concepts
Communication	Adaptability	Change
Creative	Commitment	Design
Decision-making	Consideration	Energy
Imaginative	Co-operation	Language
Numerical	Curiosity	Living things
Observational	Empathy	Love
Organisational	Perseverance	Matter
Physical	Self-confidence	Number
Problem-solving	Self-discipline	Society
Social	Tolerance	Time

(Other titles may be used.)

You will also need

(1) Five blank cards for each set (total of 15 cards for each set)

(2) Fifteen blank cards for a set of knowledge cards for which there are no predetermined titles

(3) A square board with sides of 100 cm and designed as follows

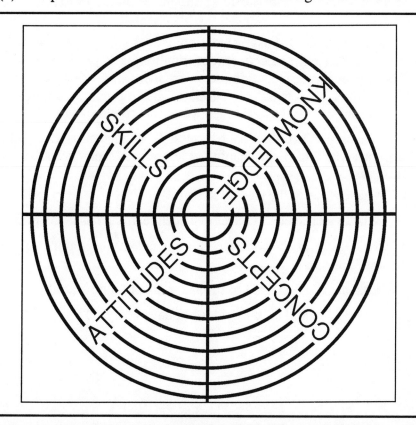

You divide the staff into departmental or inter-departmental groups. Each group will have discussions and then arrange each set of cards into the appropriate segment on the board putting the objective considered most important at the centre and working outwards to the least important one. Any objective considered inappropriate may be replaced by one of the group's own objectives written on one of the blank cards.

The groups should determine what essential knowledge needs to be taught to the students so that specific institutional aims can be achieved as distinguished from the knowledge which provides a vehicle for achieving other objectives. In other words, it may be possible within a History programme to select one example from a series to develop an understanding of the notion of 'revolution'.

The board game is a useful instrument for in-service development and can usually stimulate discussion.

After specifying institutional and departmental-level curriculum objectives for realising the overall aims, individual teachers must then devise learning activities and experiences to reflect and promote these aims and objectives. The relationship between such curriculum discussions and profiling should be much clearer by this stage.

It is important that the assessment objectives should form part of a unified, consistent and coherent curriculum package. Such discussions are essential to determine *what should be assessed.* When these overall objectives are translated into specific teaching and learning objectives, the assessment picture becomes even clearer.

The question 'What should be assessed?' is then related to other questions which have the shaping of learning as their central theme. These are

(1) What do I want the student to learn?

(2) What evidence can I collect that such learning has taken place?

(3) What does such evidence tell me about the nature of this learning?

(4) What decisions ought I to be taking about future learning?

(5) How do I record all the evidence I have collected?

(6) How do I communicate the evidence to students and discuss it with them?

(7) What does such evidence tell me about my teaching and the curriculum objectives?

The Curriculum from 5–16 Curriculum Matters 2 put these questions in another way:

'If schools are to fulfil these aims of assessment, development is needed in three main areas: clearer definition of expectations as expressed through the aims and objectives of curricula and schemes of work; improved methods of assessment in the classroom on a day to day basis; and improved methods of recording and reporting progress.

Improvement in performance must be measured against a clear identification of what it is hoped pupils will experience, learn and master. This in turn requires that the aims and objectives be known and expressed in schemes of work which set out the content, concepts, skills and attitudes to be acquired and the teaching approaches and learning resources to be used. It follows that pupils need to be given tasks which allow them to demonstrate their competence across the range of performance expected of them. In this sense the assessment process is an integral part of the curriculum.'

Relating assessment objectives to learning objectives provides the strongest possible case in support of designing profiles within an institution. The teacher in the classroom determines the learning objectives and must therefore be responsible for designing the assessment objectives so that they can be in harmony. Profiles designed within an institution are sufficiently flexible to respond to its diverse assessment objectives, the different needs and aspirations of individual students and the changing nature of the curriculum and assessment objectives.

The last point is important. A profile should never be static but should reflect and promote regular curriculum review through the information revealed. As a normal part of institutional life, assessment should therefore focus discussion on

> learning objectives of individual students
> teaching objectives
> whole curriculum objectives, and
> institutional and departmental aims

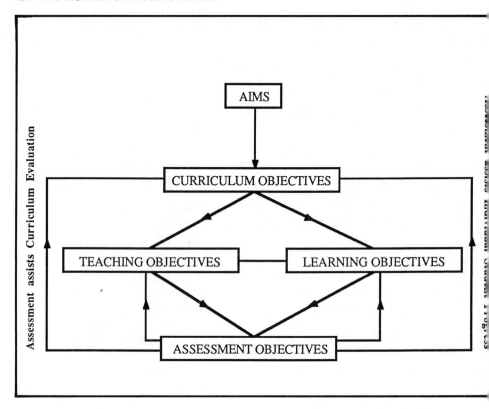

A profile can become a powerful tool for promoting curriculum evaluation and can provide important evidence within curriculum planning to help ensure that the essential characteristics of breadth, balance, relevance, differentiation, progression and continuity are maintained for individuals and groups of students.

The learning experiences of the students may not in practice cover the same breadth and balance as the original intentions. This may be particularly so for some who may be in danger of receiving an impoverished curriculum because of learning difficulties and the provision of appropriate remedial assistance. Breadth and balance must also be provided *within* curriculum areas just as much as *between* curriculum areas. You may find the following areas suggested by HMI a useful guide for determining what your curriculum should provide

Aesthetic and creative
Human and social
Linguistic and literary
Mathematic
Moral
Physical
Scientific
Spiritual
Technological

The information generated by a well-designed institutional profile tied to curriculum objectives can also help significantly in resolving problems relating to relevance, progression and continuity in student learning. Examples of this are

(1) It can help to ensure that curriculum provision is tied more directly to individual needs by taking account both of past experiences and future needs

(2) It can facilitate learning styles based on individual programmes rather than groups created by setting and banding

(3) It can facilitate continuity of learning and teaching when students are transferred within and between institutions.

The development of an institutional profile may provide the only opportunity for individual teachers and institutions to ensure that all learning experiences are ordered so as to facilitate pupils' progress in such a way that successive elements make appropriate demands and lead to better performance.

IMPLICATIONS FOR PASTORAL AND GUIDANCE SYSTEMS

An institution's academic and pastoral structures often operate independently of each other. The development of a profile scheme can provide cohesion and mutual support by integrating the curriculum, the pastoral structure and the recording and reporting systems.

The relationship between students and staff is crucial for the effective development of a profiling system. The students must be seen as central to the process and must therefore become real partners in the learning and assessment procedures which exist for their benefit.

If the main aim of the scheme of profile assessment is to help students to learn, the institution's structure must provide support to enable this to occur. Some of the most significant requirements will be

Facilities for the staff of individual departments to discuss the curriculum objectives regularly and fully

The response of individual students to these objectives

The action required to ensure progression

In some profiling schemes teachers spend too much valuable time in completing forms and too little in providing feedback to the students. This balance must be wrong. The documentation exists to provide information which can be communicated to the student; it is the discussion which is important. The only way that this can occur effectively is to change the management of teaching and learning. Time for teacher assessment, recording, reporting and counselling must be built into the institutional programme but emphasis must also be given to providing opportunities for effective discussion of individual student performance when learning activities take place.

But this does not solve the problem of enabling the student to interpret and evaluate the whole curriculum package. Every student has a 'tutor' who takes personal responsibility for monitoring academic, personal and social development and should also play a key role in the profiling process. He or she is well placed to establish the necessary relationship with the student for giving effective guidance. The tutor can help the student to understand the total education provision by

Reviewing all departmental and course assessment
Evaluating recurrent weaknesses
Recognising particular strengths
Celebrating achievements and successes
Appraising future needs and goals

The tutor is also well placed to take responsibility for the assessment and the recording of particular profile components. The tutor would not make the assessments alone but would take responsibility for collating them and would interpret and evaluate the varied responses with the student. In particular, the tutor could play a significant role in those sections of the profile relating to cross-curricular skills, personal and social skills and achievements and experiences.

In profiling the pastoral system is very important and the tutor is vital to the student. Although bringing together the academic and pastoral structures of the institution will produce enormous advantages, this central role of the pastoral system will have significant implications.

Implications for staff and student relationships and responsibilities

Relationships between students and staff and between academic and pastoral staff will be affected together with their respective responsibilities. A process involving the student as an effective partner will fundamentally challenge the traditional teacher-student relationships. These new relationships must evolve gradually if both staff and students are to maintain confidence. A process involving discussion and, possibly, negotiation and joint decision making will not be familiar to students and teachers, and care must be taken to avoid unnecessary confusion and anxiety. The Careers and Counselling Development Unit at the University of Leeds has produced the following summary of possible relationships between students and teachers, which may be useful when considering how student involvement can be improved.

Teacher decides
Teacher diagnoses – Teacher decides
Teacher diagnoses – Feedback   – Teacher decides
Teacher diagnoses – Feedback   – Discusses   – Teacher decides
Teacher diagnoses – Feedback   – Negotiates   – Joint decision
Teacher diagnoses – Feedback   – Student decides
Student discusses   – Student diagnoses – Student decides
Student decides

Whichever level of involvement is used, the relationship between teacher and student must be based on mutual trust, respect and dignity.

The relationships between members of staff are also likely to be changed if the tutor takes on the kind of central role outlined earlier. This would mean more co-operation between staff at different levels so that assessment might specifically assist the student.

Implications for the tutorial programme

The central role of the pastoral system in the profile process will affect the organisation and content of the tutorial programme. Tutors' involvement in the traditional academic structure and the learning objectives will reduce the time available to them and to any structured tutorial programme for promoting personal and social education.

Implications for pastoral staff

The central importance of the student's personal tutor will affect the traditional responsibilities of the tutor, the year or house head and the deputy head responsible for the pastoral system. There will be similar implications for colleges of further education in relation to their counselling and guidance systems.

IMPLICATIONS FOR RECORDING AND REPORTING SYSTEMS

A profiling system must form the basis of the recording and reporting system in a school or college. No teacher will want to operate a profiling system in addition to traditional mark books, internal recording systems and parental report systems so these must be included within the profiling process.

If profiles are to be available to students and parents, you may wish to maintain for each student a confidential file containing the minimum of information.

To be effective, profiling documentation should be immediately available to teachers, students and parents for updating or consultation. This suggests that the documents ought to be maintained by subject teachers and the form tutor rather than being stored inaccessibly in a Year Head's filing cabinet.

A carefully designed profile system can form the basis of a reporting system for parents. It would provide them with far more detailed information than they have traditionally received about progress, attainment, achievements and specific learning difficulties.

A profiling system should also provide information for use by people such as school careers officers, educational welfare officers and employers who need to have access to or make use of school records. Profiles ought to serve their needs without further records but they are unlikely ever to take the place of confidential references.

A profile scheme will always be most valuable for the student and the teacher by monitoring progress on a continuous and flexible basis and permitting speedy and well-informed remedial action to be taken. But this is where practical difficulties occur. The amount of detail which is recorded must compromise between what the student needs for the learning process and what the teacher can manage. Collecting and recording too much information which will never be used is as dangerous as having too little. At first there must be caution until teachers are confident and familiar with new developments and are satisfied that they will not place undue burdens on the scheme's administration and operation. The staff must decide what is critical information for recording and reporting, even though this might mean omitting valuable information.

The practical problems of profiling are dealt with in the next chapter. The implementation of any scheme of profile assessment will have considerable implications which must be anticipated so that the direction, quality and pace of change can be planned.

Chapter 9

PRACTICAL CONSIDERATIONS

One of the major arguments in favour of designing a profile for a specific school or college is that it can take account of the practical problems which apply to that particular place. The nature of the management and structure of an individual organisation will affect the design and operation of its profile and the curriculum will affect its content. All kinds of practical considerations will be relevant: the amount of available tutorial time, printing facilities, computer technology, clerical support or the ways in which staff-student ratios are used to affect contact time.

The practical problems will vary from place to place but there are certain difficulties which always occur. These are

Preparation
Time
Cost
Expertise

PREPARATION

Teaching staff must become competent in profiling tasks and other important partners in the process must also be prepared.

Fundamental changes in the structure and operation of institutions cannot be undertaken without preparatory work with the students. This will be especially crucial if the process is introduced where students have had experience of different approaches and relationships. They need to understand the processes and have confidence in them if they are to make effective contributions. Self-evaluation skills do not happen automatically and these will have to be developed.

Parents must be informed about the principles and practices of profiling so that they can understand the changes to the school or college system. This will be a demanding task but it is particularly important to gain their support as important partners in the process. They must understand the reasons for the changes and the effects these will have on the evaluation of student progress and achievements. They will need to be made aware of the implications of changes in recording their own children's progress and achievements. These could, for example, affect

The marking of exercise books
The nature of consultation evenings
The existence of interviews between teachers and children, and
The nature of the communications between school or college and home

Employers must also be involved in any preparation programme. The development of national records of achievement may lead the government and LEAs to embark on a broad educational programme to inform employers of the nature and purpose of these schemes, but such a publicity campaign may not have a great impact locally and may not be noticed by many small employers. A school will therefore benefit from considering how such people can be informed of developments and what the implications may be for transferring from school to employment or for the provision of Work Experience.

Changes may also affect the local community which ought to be made aware of such large-scale developments. The governors may play a crucial role in preparing the community for the full-scale implementation of such schemes. The whole basis of the accountability of an institution may indeed be changed.

TIME

This is the most common problem raised by teachers who operate or are about to introduce schemes of profile assessment. The burdens on teachers increase year by year particularly in administration. Profile assessment should be seen as an indispensible aid to teaching and learning rather than another administrative chore. It should be the means for bringing together all aspects of the curriculum by the provision of a focus for curriculum development, course planning and evaluation, the monitoring of student progress and achievements and the discussion of these with students and their parents.

In this way less time might be taken up than would be the case if all these activities had been separately planned and evaluated. Profiling should be regarded as a development which supports rather than hinders the work of the teacher and the institution.

Consideration must be given to

the time needed to undertake the planning and design stages, and

redistributing the use of time when the scheme is implemented.

Time for design

There are a number of ways of finding additional time for planning. They include

(1) Reappraisal of timetabling to provide departmental discussion time

(2) Review of the nature and structure of the school day, and

(3) More flexible arrangements concerning staff contact time and the organisation of student teaching groups.

It may be beneficial to accommodate short-term inconveniences for the sake of long-term advantages.

The scheme in operation

Consideration must be given to

the effects on classroom teaching, and

the administration of the scheme.

Caution has already been urged in the demands that teachers make of themselves in the early stages; more can be achieved as experience and expertise is gained. A profile should provide for every student a cumulative picture emerging over a period and revealing a developing image of strengths and weaknesses rather than an immediate snapshot of attainment and abilities. We believe that the most valuable assessment takes place in the classroom and this should be encouraged wherever possible. This will inevitably influence the choice of recording method to be used when a judgement is made during the teaching process. Information gained then could, however, be recorded later by a different method for use in discussion with individual students or their parents.

It is also important to specify the learning objectives clearly because this will lead to easier assessment and recording: the more generalised the learning objectives, the more time-consuming the assessment process.

You may not think that much of this has anything to do with time but it has. Time is most likely to be found through changes in classroom and institutional management. What kinds of change in the classroom might produce the time and space needed to operate the profiling process more successfully?

Changes in Classroom Management
(1) The necessary strategies for learning, assessment, feedback, negotiation and remedial action are unlikely to be achieved by a didactic, chalk-and-talk approach to teaching. A shift towards *individualised learning* will lead to individualised assessment and recording without which individual progress cannot be monitored.

(2) The evidence for the crucial dialogue between teacher and student might be provided from *self-assessment* or *peer-assessment* as part of a group activity. This *shift of responsibility on to the student* for providing the evidence has interesting implications for time and other benefits may well accrue from students' increased self-awareness and responsibility.

(3) There needs to be a *rigorous review of curriculum content.* Curriculum review and reappraisal as outlined earlier, combined with the joint planning of curriculum and assessment objectives, should reveal areas where time and space can be found. This requires the identification of outdated, inappropriate, irrelevant or duplicated content and unstructured repetition of the same skills or attitudes. Such a review is also likely to lead to a more unified curriculum and assessment package.

You may well wonder whether such answers can apply to the overcrowded examination years. We believe that they can and must. A rigorous analysis of examination syllabuses can often reveal duplication of content and repetition of the same skills. The development of subject-specific and general criteria within GCSE and, ultimately, the development of criteria related to grades should help the design of courses, avoid undue emphasis on the acquisition of knowledge and prevent unnecessary repetition. Moreover, an individualised approach to learning is as meaningful to students involved in the examination years as it is to any other students.

Administration of the Scheme

This is another aspect concerning time. However much emphasis is put on discussion with students, time has to be found for the collation of various assessments and records. It is difficult to be precise about how this might be achieved because each school or college has its own administrative structure, but it may be useful to deal with some areas which will need to be considered.

In many places, tutorial time may have to be extended if there is to be regular discussion with the students. The pressures may vary throughout the year and consideration will have to be given as to how to build flexibility into the system.

There are a number of ways of doing this.
(1) A tutor could have counselling periods in his or her timetable and students could be withdrawn from their normal activities.
(2) Groups could join each other and be flexible in size to release tutors for interview.
(3) There could be a relief tutor.
(4) Occasional changes could be made to the structure of the school day.

The profile must become the cornerstone of the recording and reporting system. In some places time might be saved by bringing together different records and reports into a unified process. Some teachers spend many hours transferring information from one document to another. Duplication is one of the biggest time-wasters and during the design period it will be important to ensure that the system will cater for all the needs of the institution.

Eventually, the increased use of information technology in schools and colleges will really benefit data storage and retrieval but it must respond to the needs of the institution rather than dictate particular approaches to assessment and recording.

COST

The most expensive item in profiling will almost certainly be staff time. Most printing departments are probably equipped to produce the documents needed for the internal recording of student progress and achievements. If the development is given a high priority it ought to be possible to recover the small cost involved from capitation allowances.

It may be important to ensure that documents are of a high quality particularly when they are intended for parents and employers but time and money ought to be spent mainly on the use of any document rather than the document itself.

You may believe that the summative record of achievement should be well produced to help its credibility. This should be discussed with the governors and the LEA. It may be possible to consider some form of sponsorship or to reallocate some money used for examination fees.

We do not want to underestimate the problem of cost, but it can be solved so that many schools and colleges can operate profile systems using attractive documents which they can produce comparatively cheaply.

EXPERTISE

Staff expertise and confidence are important to the development of profiling. There is considerably more expertise about than may at first be realised. It needs to be harnessed, developed and used for the benefit of all. There must be mutual trust and a willingness to learn from one another.

The skills needed are diverse but do exist. There may be some teachers who have already developed skills in designing tasks which can promote and provide evidence for specific criteria. There may be some who have developed methods of assessment for various situations. There may be some who are already skilled in accurate reporting of student performance. All these skills must be systematically discovered and a programme devised for gradually passing them on to others. Skills that are needed but do not exist must also be identified.

Some probable areas needing in-service development are

(1) Identifying the assessment criteria at departmental and institutional levels

(2) Developing assessment techniques for each of the criteria

(3) Developing appropriate methods of recording progress and achievements

(4) Developing the necessary reporting skills for conveying assessment results to a variety of audiences

(5) Developing the necessary counselling and negotiation skills for communicating effectively with students and deciding together future courses of action

An individual school or college may, of course, have other needs. Help in dealing with them may be found from various sources. The list opposite is by no means exhaustive but provides pointers towards further assistance.

You may also find the services of the National Profiling Network useful. The Network gives profiling information, expertise and experiences to its members. It has a large amount of information on current profiling practice. Its address is given on page 5.

The reader may discover useful information from the nine pilot projects funded by the DES to assist in the design of the national guidelines for the implementation of records of achievement.

These are

Dorset	Lancashire
Essex	Suffolk
ILEA	Wigan

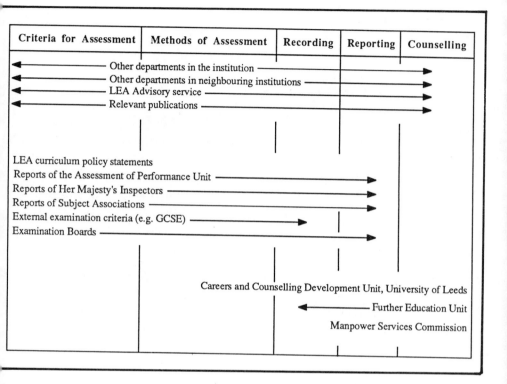

Criteria for Assessment	Methods of Assessment	Recording	Reporting	Counselling

Other departments in the institution

Other departments in neighbouring institutions

LEA Advisory service

Relevant publications

LEA curriculum policy statements

Reports of the Assessment of Performance Unit

Reports of Her Majesty's Inspectors

Reports of Subject Associations

External examination criteria (e.g. GCSE)

Examination Boards

Careers and Counselling Development Unit, University of Leeds

Further Education Unit

Manpower Services Commission

The East Midlands Examining Group with Derbyshire, Lincolnshire, Nottinghamshire and Northamptonshire

The Oxford Certificate of Educational Achievement with Coventry, Leicestershire, Oxfordshire and Somerset

The Welsh Joint Education Committee

Staff confidence will increase when it is seen how profiling can help teachers. The importance of assessment is not emphasised in student teachers' courses and so their assessment skills are undeveloped. Once these skills are developed and teachers can see that being able to use an increased range of assessment techniques makes them more effective, they will continue confidently.

Chapter **10**

CONCLUSION

A great problem in writing a book like this is to find a balance between making the development and operation of profiles seem relatively simple and straightforward and making them seem too difficult and complicated and so not worth attempting. Plenty of down-to-earth advice must be provided, which is neither simplistic nor patronising. At the same time, it has to be stressed that such advice can only be acted on within a carefully planned and conceptually rigorous framework.

Designing an institutional profile is a very demanding task but it is one that is within the competence of any school or college staff provided that the will is there. A well-designed profile can substantially improve the quality of the whole teaching/learning experience for everyone. These benefits are, however, very much related to the amount of time, thought and energy devoted to the preparation of the profile particularly in the early stages of its development. This inevitably places a major strain on teachers as individuals and as a group, and central and local governments need to recognise how important it is to provide for staff development in this area. When morale and resources are low this will not be easy. Profiling (the process) and profiles or records of achievement (the product) are, however, among the few current initiatives that promote curriculum unity rather than curriculum division, particularly for students aged between 14 and 19. There are enormous potential benefits for students, teachers, parents, employers and the community at large. We hope that this book has managed to highlight these benefits and to show how they can be realistically achieved in practice in both the short and the long term.

READING LIST

CSE Mode 3 and the Humanities Project	A. Dale and J. Elliot (eds)	Humanities Curriculum Project 1972
Assessment in Education	D. J. Lewis	Hodder & Stoughton 1974
Record of Personal Experience Qualities & Qualifications (Tutor's Handbook)	D. Stansbury	RPE Publications South Brent, Devon 1975
Assessment and Testing in Secondary Schools	R. N. Deale Schools Council Examinations Bulletin 32	Evans/Methuen Educational 1975
The Whole Curriculum 13–16	Schools Council Working Paper 53	Evans/Methuen Educational 1975
Making the Most of Teachers' Knowledge of Pupils	Scottish Pupil Profile Project	The Scottish Council for Research in Education Hodder & Stoughton 1977
Assessing Students: How shall we know them?	D. Rowntree	Harper & Row 1977
Pupils in Profile	Scottish Headteachers	The Scottish Council for Research in Education Hodder & Stoughton 1977
Assessment in the Affective Domain	W. B. Dockrell & H. B. Black	The Scottish Council for Research in Education Hodder & Stoughton 1978
Assessment,Schools and Society	P. Broadfoot	Methuen 1979
Record of Personal Achievement: An independent evaluation	T. Swales	Schools Council Pamphlet 16 1979
Diamond Challenge Scheme	D. Stansbury	Springline Trust, Totnes 1979
In-School Evaluation	M. Shipman	Heinemann 1979

Outcomes of Education	T. Burgess & E. Adams (eds)	Macmillan Education 1980
What do they know: a Review of Criteria-referenced assessment	S. Brown	HMSO Edinburgh 1980
Records of Achievement	G. Pearson	Schools Council News 1981
Trainee Centred Reviewing (TCR) Helping trainees to help themselves	B. Pearce et al.	Manpower Services Commission Research and Development Series No.2 1981
Can Do Cards and Profiles	M. Freshwater & N. Oates	Manpower Services Commission 1981
Assessment in Schools	D. Satterley	Blackwell 1981
The Practical Curriculum	Schools Council Working Paper 70	Methuen Educational 1981
Curriculum in Action: An Approach to Education- Block 6, Measuring Learning Outcomes	Open University/ Schools Council	Open University Press 1981
Profile Reports for School Leavers	J. Balogh	Schools Council Longmans 1982
Profiles, a review of issues and practices in the use and development of Profiles		Futher Education Unit/ Department of Education and Science 1982
Record keeping and Profiles Guidance to Schools	P. & J. Mortimore	Inner London Education Authority 1982
Diagnostic Assessment in Secondary Schools	H. B. Black & W. B. Dockrell	The Scottish Council for Research in Education 1982
Keeping track of teaching	H. B. Black & P. Broadfoot	Routledge & Kegan Paul 1982
Assessment in Youth Training - Made to Measure	I. Stronach et al.	Scottish Vocational Preparation Unit, Jordanhill College of Education 1982

MSC Training Studies: *Basic Skills Analysis*	M. Freshwater	Manpower Services Commission 1982
Personal and Social Education in Secondary Schools	K. David	Schools Council 1982
Pupils Personal Records: a Teachers Handbook	R. de Groot	PPR Development Group Bath University 1982
Combining Teacher Assessment with Examining Board Assessment	Seminar Report	Associated Examining Board 1982
Pupil Profiles: Policy Statement		National Association of Schoolmasters/Union of Women Teachers 1982
Assessment in Youth Training: Made to Measure?	Scottish Vocational Preparation Unit	Jordanhill College of Education 1982
Profile Assessment: Recording Student Progress (a School focused INSET Manual)	D. Garforth	Dorset County Council, 1983 (available from West Dorset Teachers' Centre)
Records of Achievement at 16: some examples of current practice	HMI	Department of Education and Science 1983
Pupil Profiles: a discussion document		National Union of Teachers 1983
Recording Achievement at 16 plus	B. Goacher	Schools Council Longmans 1983
Profile Reporting of Examination Results	A. Harrison Schools Council Examinations Bulletin 43	Evans/Methuen Educational 1983
Profile Reporting in Wales: a discussion paper	J. Jones	Schools Council for Wales 1983
Profile Reporting System Handbook		City and Guilds of London Institute 1983
An Evaluation of a Basic Abilities Profiling System (Final Report of CGLI Project 3)	N. Stratton	City and Guilds of London Institute 1983

Computer aided Profiling	B. Maxfield	Further Education Unit/ Department of Education and Science 1983
OCEA Newsletters 1-4		Oxford Delegacy of Local Examinations 1983-84
Profiles	G. Hitchcock	Avon LEA 1984
Pupils' Personal Records: a Handbook	PPR Management Group	Bath University 1984
A Teachers Guide to Assessment	H. G. Macintosh & D. S. Frith	International Association for Educational Assessment 1984
Records of Achievement: A Statement of Policy		Department of Education and Science 1984
South Western Profile Assessment Research Project		South Western Examinations Board 1984
The Uses and Abuses of Profiling	W. Law	Harper & Row 1984 £7.95
Improving Secondary Schools	Hargreaves Report	Inner London Education Authority 1984
Profiles- An Introduction	P. Davies	Welsh Joint Education Committee 1984
Practical Skills Profiling Schemes		Royal Society of Arts 1984
School Reports to Parents	B. Goacher & M. Reid	National Foundation for Educational Research 1984
Principles of Personal Recording	D. Stansbury	Springline Trust 1984
Criterion Referenced Assessment in the Classroom	H. Black & W. B. Dockrell	The Scottish Council for Research in Education 1984
Profiles: an Annotated Bibliography	P. Broadfoot et al.	University of Bristol School of Education 1984
Profiles in Action	Ed. J. Mortimore	Further Education Unit/ Department of Education and Science 1984

Assessing Pupils: A study of Policy and Practice	E. A. Clough & P. Davis with R. Sumner	NFER Nelson 1984
Dorset/SREB Assessment & Profiling Project: Discussion Document No.1		Southern Regional Examinations Board 1985
Guideline for Descriptive Assessment	D. Suggitt	Schools & Curriculum Unit, Victorian Institute of Secondary Education 1985
Profiles and Records of Achievement: A Review of Issues and Practice	P. Broadfoot	Holt 1986
Profiles and Profiling: A Practical Introduction	G. Hitchcock	Longmans 1986

REFERENCES IN CHAPTER 7

p.85 G. Withers and G. Cornish 1984. 'Assessment in Practice: Competitive or Non-Competitive?' Occasional Paper No. 11, VISE, Melbourne.

p.99 A. Dale and J. Elliott (eds.) 1972. *CSE Mode 3 and the Humanities Curriculum Project* pp.51–6. The Humanities Curriculum Project, Norwich.